This book is given

in honor of
Chris Jones
by
Margaret Jones
May 1998

Planning and Community Equity

A Component of APA's
Agenda for America's Communities Program

PLANNERS PRESS
AMERICAN PLANNING ASSOCIATION
Chicago, Illinois   Washington, D.C.

Copyright 1994 by the American Planning Association
1313 E. 60th St., Chicago, IL 60637
Paperback edition ISBN 1-884829-05-8
Hardbound edition ISBN 1-884829-04-x
Library of Congress Catalog Number 94-72240

Printed in the United States of America

Contents

Acknowledgments

APA could not have produced this book without the extensive work, advice, and effort of a lot of people who freely gave their volunteer time to the project.

The project was initiated by the APA Board of Directors at its spring 1992 meeting under the leadership of Connie Cooper, APA president. The Board appointed a scoping task force that met during the summer of 1992 to determine how APA could respond to issues of community equity. The task force, chaired by Carol D. Barrett, had a membership consisting of Larry Allen, Robert Becker, Emerson Bryan, Eugene Grigsby, and William Lamont. In addition Connie Cooper and Janet Ruggiero meet with the committee as observers. The staff that participated included Israel Stollman, George Marcou, and Frank S. So.

As the project kicked off, the scoping task force disbanded and an Agenda for America's Communities Steering Committee was created, chaired by Janet Ruggiero. Its members included Eugene Grigsby, Oliver Byrum, Chris McGetrick, Rebecca Cedillo, and Angela Harper. In the fall of 1993, Sergio Rodriguez was appointed chair of the committee, and David Long and Ramona Mullahey were added as members.

As drafts of the chapters of this book were prepared they were reviewed by the entire APA leadership, including the Board of Directors, the AICP Commission, the Chapter Presidents Council, the Divisions Council, and the Student Representatives Council. We especially want to thank the following individuals for their careful reading of and extensive comments on individual chapters: Richard A. Maltby, Bill Ziebron, Jeff Goldman, Joanne Garnett, Sumner Sharpe, Dennis Gordon, Stephan Edson, G.L. Yolton, Jr., Nathaniel W. Karns, Gary Lozano, Mitzi Barker, Susanne S. Quarterman, Barry Seymour, Louise Mercuro, Paul J. Grasewicz, William J. Ernst, III, Martin Gallent, Barbara Becker, Ralph R. Willmer, Michael Wozniak, Dale B. Thoma, Marshall D. Slagle, Price T. Banks, Robin McClelland, Mary Kihl, David C. Slater, Debra W. Campbell, Carole Bloom, Joseph W. McManus, Clark Turner, Jose R.

Casanova, Paul S. Tischler, Steven A. Preston, Margaret Munsey, Hal Freshley, Janet R. Muchnik, John McClain, Adrian P. Freund, Margot W. Garcia, Daniel Lauber, Arlan Colton, Sam Casella, Paul Bergman, Richard C. Bernhardt, William M. Harris, Sr., Veronica Beatty, Donald L. Elliott, Norman Krumholz, Mark Hinshaw, Vanessa Akins, and Sarah More.

The Steering Committee was assisted by Frank S. So, who also coordinated the entire book project. Editorial services were provided by Jim Hecimovich and Cynthia Cheski. Sylvia Lewis coordinated the production and publishing process.

Finally, we wish to thank those who created this book—the authors of the individual chapters, all of whom volunteered their time.

Introduction

APA is proposing a vision of a "new comprehensiveness" for planning by expanding the goals of comprehensive planning to explicitly include the concept of community equity. We define community equity as the expansion of opportunities for betterment that are available to those communities most in need of them, creating more choices for those who have few. An equitable society that produces fairness for all has long been part of the planning vision, but a part that has been poorly attained. We are, therefore, restating our vision as a challenge to be met by planners and planning agencies in the conduct of community planning.

Planners have the tools at hand to create better communities. It is our professional and ethical responsibility to use these tools to produce results that are fair to all members of the American community. Fairness requires expanding the opportunities for betterment that are available to those communities most in need of them. Fairness requires creating more choices for those who have few. Fairness requires that we reduce inequalities, that we narrow the gap opened by disparities in the distribution of resources. We in the planning profession must recognize that planning decisions do influence the social and economic well-being of communities. Today, our challenges are to seek equity and fairness in the rebuilding of inner-city areas, in the development of suburban communities, and in the growth of small towns and rural areas.

"Comprehensive" has meant looking at the connections between land-use and transportation, between housing and open space, between environmental protection and economic development. We have thought of these elements as physical planning. But we have also known that physical planning has social purposes and social consequences. We can no longer plan effectively without taking account of still more connections: to education, to poverty, to public safety. We need to expand our concerns if we are to do our jobs well.

Why attempt this now? In the spring of 1992, the board of directors of the American Planning Association was shocked by the riots that took place in Los Angeles. It began a serious discussion about the implications of the riots on the practice of planning. At the same time, the national election campaigns were already underway, and there was a sense that a new period was beginning when the nation would be turning its attention to new ideas about welfare reform, health care reform, the criminal justice system, transportation policy, economic development policy, and education reform. All these areas of public policy in part play out within cities and metropolitan areas. In general, these policy areas do not directly involve urban planners to any great extent, but it is also true that what our nation, states, and cities do in these areas have profound impacts in urban areas. As planners prepare comprehensive plans and neighborhood plans, we will, and must, pay far more attention to these evolving policies and how they affect what we have traditionally done. To be truly comprehensive, we'll need to bring in more social and economic issues into our analysis and plan making. We may be bringing specialists from other fields into our planning agencies or hiring them as consultants. We will certainly be interacting with other agencies responsible for social and economic programs.

As APA began its assessment of the planning field, we were reminded about how the nation had faced the social and economic problems of cities in the past.

> The new decade brings an old challenge to the urban professions: the challenge of change. . . . [The] old policies, the old ways of thinking, and the old institutions are not responsive to the crucial needs of today. The problems . . . center around divisiveness in metropolitan areas along social and economic lines. Too many Americans are becoming alienated not only from each other but from the institutions of representative democracy. . . . The problems of rural America are not too different from central city problems.

These words were written by the late Samuel C. Jackson when he was General Assistant Secretary of HUD in 1970, two years after the Kerner Commission's conclusion that we were "moving toward two societies, one black, one white—separate and unequal." Jackson described his concerns about housing and transportation and jobs and schools and drug addiction and crime. He called it an old challenge in 1970. Today, it is a generation older and a generation more urgent.

Two books published in 1992 note, by their very titles, that, for all the change of two and a half decades, we must deal with the problems of two societies still. One was written by APA members William Goldsmith and Edward Blakely: *Separate Societies: Poverty and Inequality in U.S. Cities.* The other is by Andrew Hacker: *Two Nations: Black and White, Separate, Hostile, Unequal.* Clearly, we still have the same problems, only they have become worse.

Are we now prepared to meet the challenge more successfully? We will be if we accept community equity as an essential component of planning and demonstrate how community planning enhances community equity and is important to the achievement of other community goals. As community planners, we draw strength from our adherence to principles that we share. We believe that today's decisions must be made with thought not only to their short-term effect but also to their long-range consequences. What will such decisions do for my children? And for your children? We believe in looking comprehensively at the impacts that solutions for different problems have on each other. And we must believe in a society that draws strength from values that are shared across the full range of our diverse population, including the value of community equity.

For people who live in most inner cities and in many rural areas, the quality of life is often severely depressed and opportunities for betterment are scanty. The key problems that planners currently address—housing, transportation, economic development, environmental protection, land-use decisions, capital improvements—have a critical bearing on that quality of life. The decisions that planners make, the proposals that planners prepare in these areas of professional practice, have a potent impact in establishing levels of quality and opportunity. In a planning context, the objective of community equity is to reduce the inequalities of results, to narrow the gap when disparities have been created in the distribution of goods and services influenced by planning decisions.

We recognize more than we did in the past that we cannot distinguish physical planning from social. Physical planning has social purposes and social consequences just as it has environmental purposes and environmental consequences; just as it has fiscal purposes and fiscal consequences. The planning profession has long recognized its obligations to community equity. APA's Articles of Incorporation state that we:

. . . are organized to advance the art and science of planning—physical, economic, and social—at the local, regional, state, and national levels. The objective of the Association is to encourage planning that will contribute to public well being by developing communities and environments that meet more effectively the needs of people and of society.

The AICP Code of Ethics and Professional Conduct, which is also a part of APA's statement of Ethical Principles in Planning, requires that:

A planner must strive to expand choice and opportunity for all persons, recognizing a special responsibility to plan for the needs of disadvantaged groups and persons, and must urge the alteration of policies, institutions and decisions which oppose such needs.

Achieving equitable results in planning is also a continuing responsibility that future generations of planners must undertake. The schools that teach planning have appropriately committed themselves to transmit this obligation. The guidelines for the accreditation of planning programs include the following among components of a curriculum:

Students must be able to identify and debate the importance and effects of the following values in relation to actual planning issues: (1) Issues of equity, social justice, economic welfare, and efficiency in the use of resources. (2) The role of government and citizen participation in a democratic society and in the balancing of individual and collective rights and interests. (3) Respect for diversity of views and ideologies. . . .

The challenge to pursue our principles effectively is greater now than it was a generation ago. Our cities have experienced an increasing concentration of social ills and economic decay. A major cause of the current urban condition is the rapid revolution in technology and economy. This has occurred against a background of a slower evolution in positive race relations. If racist barriers to economic opportunity had been removed in the older economy of manufacturing jobs and clerks with pencils, we would likely have achieved a smoother transition to an equitable society. But an enormous gap has opened between the effective education and training of racial minorities and the demands of the technologically oriented workplace. The globalizing economy demands higher skill and knowledge levels of our people. Effective solutions to these problems are hampered by lingering racism from the age when it was legally sanctioned and new racism that continues to foster separateness.

Our professional responsibility to help create good communities requires attention to community equity in the distribution of resources, especially in an era of resource scarcity. We cannot, for long, have healthy, prosperous communities that are insulated from impoverished ones. While some suburban economies have grown increasingly independent of central cities, those that have done best have central cities that are also doing well. Smaller cities and towns are already coping with similar versions of what are now inner-city problems. We must plan on the basis of even greater interdependence at metropolitan, state, and national levels. A fractured society cannot compete in a global economy.

Our role as planners is to address equity issues through the plans, policies, and programs that we now prepare. Every topic that we touch has elements that will affect results and influence the allocation of resources that it may take to make them equitable. A new approach to comprehensiveness in planning will not separate the analyses we make of economic impacts, fiscal impacts, and environmental impacts, but will include social impacts and examine them together as a whole so that all parts will mutually reinforce a proposed plan and not, through cross-purposes, defeat it.

Our role nationally is to provide a continuing stream of technical advice, case examples, and informational support for a reinvigorated approach to a new comprehensiveness in planning. Even the best planning will not resolve all equity issues quickly. Our challenge is to establish a direction and a systematic ongoing program that fosters our inventiveness as a caring and effective profession contributing to the overall health of the American community.

The purpose of this book is to begin the process of providing direction to the field by presenting a series of papers designed to stimulate thinking about planning practice. Some of the papers deal with traditional planning topics such as housing, transportation, and citizen participation, and emphasize how such planning can be focused on community equity concerns. Other papers, such as education or human services, present topics that planners don't currently work in very much, but areas that need new attention by planners. Each paper discusses and presents opportunities to integrate community equity objectives in our plans. The papers recognize that there are not universally apt prescriptions that fit every community and every political context. Our hope is that these papers suggest yet additional ideas, approaches, techniques, and planning tools that may be adapted to pursue our objectives.

1

Affordable Housing:
Decent Shelter Is a Fundamental Right

By S. Mark White and Jim Hecimovich

As recently as 25 years ago, national housing policy focused on the provision of public housing in inner cities as *the* affordable housing issue. Urban renewal attempted to remedy simultaneously both the social effects of racial discrimination and poverty and the physical decay of central city neighborhoods. While those problems remain and have, in fact, worsened, there have been two significant additions to the affordable housing issue that have put it firmly back in the spotlight of mainstream America and called for a new policy. The "American dream" of homeownership is slipping beyond the reach of the middle class, while, at the same time, decent rental housing requires a greater and greater portion of family income.

The lack of affordable housing for all is also an economic development issue. Without it, employers are unlikely to locate in an area, stifling job creation and threatening job retention. Given this recognition that housing affordability is an issue that transcends racial, class, and city/suburban boundaries and is tied to economic development, there is an opportunity to craft new policies and techniques, building on the successful programs that exist and renewing the call for affordable, decent shelter for all people in this country, not as an economic privilege but as a fundamental right.

There are many causes behind the new housing affordability problem. While it has always been true that low-income families simply have not had the money to buy homes or secure better rental housing, the change to a service economy in the U.S. has now put many middle-class families in the same bind. Despite significant drops in mortgage rates, salaries paid for service economy jobs, coupled with appreciation in housing costs, make it difficult for many people to come up with the necessary downpayment to secure a mortgage. It is also true that saving for that downpayment takes more time and becomes more difficult when first-time homebuyers are paying high rents while looking for a house. The recession of 1991-1992 exacerbated this problem.

While the increasing cost of land, inflation, and higher construction standards have contributed to the cost of housing, there has been renewed criticism of government regulations as a primary contributor to the housing affordability problem. The title of the most recent federal criticism minces no words—*"Not in My Back Yard": Removing Barriers to Affordable Housing*. While many of the recommendations contained in the report are sound, others go too far and threaten to roll back progress made in the areas of environmental regulation, local government finance, and zoning reform.

Planners need to respond to these criticisms by offering programs that provide affordable housing *without* jeopardizing those gains or gutting those regulations. Such programs already exist. Proactive lobbying from planners at the federal, state, and local level, dissemination of information through APA's products and services, and personal commitment in the performance of one's day-to-day job can go a long way toward resolving the housing affordability problem without dismantling the regulatory system that provides numerous protections for many people. The rest of this paper looks at existing tools, offering recommendations and examples, and concludes with a review of the most effective response to the affordable housing problem—state comprehensive planning and legislation that mandates local and regional planning to produce affordable housing.

SOMETHING TO BUILD ON

The existing planning tools that can be used to resolve the affordable housing problem fall in two categories: affirmative measures and reactive measures. Affirmative measures employ land-use controls to provide affordable housing. Reactive measures target the modification of regulations so that they do not, in fact, constitute a barrier to the provision of affordable housing. Recommendations follow.

Affirmative Measures

Inclusionary zoning. Inclusionary zoning ties development approval to, or creates incentives for, the provision of low- and moderate-income housing as part of a proposed development. Many states, including California, Connecticut, Florida, Maryland, New Hampshire, and New Jersey, expressly authorize mandatory or optional inclusionary zoning programs. In optional programs, a developer can exchange the provision of low- and moderate-income for regulatory incentives (e.g., density bonuses). In mandatory programs, developers must set aside a portion of development for low- and moderate-income households.

Incentives for inclusionary zoning

Irvine, California, redesigned its inclusionary zoning program in 1991. The housing element in the city's general plan now includes incentives for builders who set aside up to 25 percent of their units for affordable housing. The units must remain affordable for 30 years, must offer a mix of sizes comparable to the market-rate units, and must be dispersed throughout the project. Ten percent must be accessible under ADA requirements. There must also be an "affirmative" marketing program for the project (e.g., local ads in Vietnamese and Spanish newspapers). In turn, development project fees are waived, financing through federal block grants and state housing bonds is made available, and below-market-rate construction loans and other "write-downs" are offered to the developer. (See Planning, February 1993, for examples of other inclusionary programs with incentives.)

Mandatory programs are more effective than optional programs, are legally defensible, and should be authorized by state enabling legislation. They can help achieve community and national goals of social and economic integration.

Linkage programs. Linkage fees require a developer to contribute a fee to a housing trust fund or to make equity contributions to a low-income housing project. The rationale is that new development attracts employees (either to work in commercial or office uses or to serve residential uses) to a region, creating greater demand for housing and inflating housing prices. Linkage fees have been successfully used in San Francisco, Boston, and Santa Monica.

Linkage fees, like impact fees, should be authorized by state enabling legislation and made defensible under the rational nexus standard. Affordable housing is as much of a part of a community's necessary public facilities as are sewers and roads. Linkage fees make certain that new development pays its fair share of the cost of those facilities.

Housing trust funds and TIF districts. Changes in the tax code and federal disinvestment in low-income housing have created a need for new ways to finance affordable housing. Housing trust funds, whose revenues can be generated from a variety of sources, are flexible tools that can be used to provide money to low- and moderate-income homebuyers and renters for purposes ranging from the production of affordable units to loan guarantees. Twenty states currently have housing trust funds.

All states should have housing trust funds; creation of a national housing trust fund that focuses on the needs of special populations (e.g., the elderly, homeless, large families) should be considered.

Tax increment financing districts are used to encourage the redevelopment of blighted areas. While TIF programs are usually reserved to promote traditional economic development activities (e.g., infrastructure improvements), California requires that 20 percent of TIF revenues be allocated for moderate-, low-, and very-low-income housing, and Minnesota authorizes the use of TIF plans in special housing districts, where they can be used to finance the housing, to pay for public improvements directly related to affordable housing projects, and to cover administrative expenses.

TIF legislation should be modified to require a portion of TIF revenues to be used to facilitate the production of affordable housing.

Promoting infill and preserving the supply of affordable housing. Infill development avoids the expensive costs related to new development, with savings found in providing services and infrastructure and a reduction in land speculation. Infill also preserves open space that might be lost to development otherwise. Infill development can be promoted through the use of techniques like *TIF districts, downzoning, density bonuses, and the elimination of overzoning for industrial uses in urban areas.*

Preservation of existing affordable housing prevents its conversion to other uses, maintaining a jurisdiction's supply of such housing and relieving pressure on that market. Many jurisdictions have adopted ordinances that use *replacement provisions and demolition licenses* to ensure the preservation of their affordable housing supply. Seattle, San Francisco, Hartford, and New York City condition the demolition of certain types of housing on the replacement of such housing elsewhere, the payment of a fee in lieu of such replacement, or the payment of relocation assistance to tenants. *Single room occupancy (SRO) ordinances* combine SRO demolition moratoria with relaxed construction standards and below-market interest loans to SRO developers to promote that type of housing. *Rent control programs* may be a viable form of preserving housing affordability in fast-growing areas, but such programs must contain protections (e.g., exempting new housing construction, fair return standards, vacancy decontrol, and monitoring the system to see that its benefits are reaching the intended audience) to ensure that they are legally defensible and that their overall effect does not negatively affect housing costs.

Infill and preservation strategies can be extremely effective when they are coupled with anti-redlining legislation (e.g., the Community Reinvestment Act) and public investment policies (e.g., the donation of tax delinquent properties) to assist in renewing decaying areas while promoting stable housing costs.

Reactive Measures

Reactive measures seek to remedy the detrimental effects of existing standards on housing affordability. Efforts should be made *now* to review a jurisdiction's overall regulatory framework and measure its effect on housing affordability. Planners will find that the combination of many of these reactive measures may be necessary to provide for the production of low- and moderate-income housing.

Zoning and subdivision reform. Regulatory reform does not mean the wholesale abdication of regulatory responsibilities; the wholesale abandonment of regulations *would do nothing to promote the production of low-income housing.* Rather, development standards should be revised by type and category of development and by geographic area. Consider the following as just two types of standards that can be revised and encouraged.

> *Density.* Increases in density can promote savings in land costs and service delivery. Higher densities should be encouraged.

> *Site standards.* Reduce minimum lot sizes overall; reduce or eliminate minimum lot sizes for PUD/cluster developments; reduce lot frontage requirements, resulting in savings in pavement, stormwater control, and utility costs; reduce front setback standards, reducing pavement, service line, site clearance, and landscaping costs; reduce street-width requirements; modify sidewalk standards and allow use of alternative paving materials; use natural stormwater management systems, reducing stormwater facility construction costs and ongoing maintenance costs.

Saving and Building SROs, from California to Richmond, Virginia . . .

Single room occupancy hotels are not popular—many were bulldozed in and around CBDs to make way for new, more lucrative projects in the 1970s and '80s. Their demolition clearly added to the problem of homelessness in many cities. San Diego's planning staff was asked to develop a strategy that would preserve SROs without dampening development in the downtown. The result—a public/private initiative that built 18 new SROs with a total of 2,262 new rooms and renovation of another nine with 388 rooms. How? Through a 1987 ordinance that required owners to replace very-low-income SRO units lost through demolition and through regulatory streamlining and financial incentives. On the regulatory side, the city reclassified SROs from multifamily to commercial, thereby eliminating numerous building (e.g., sprinkler systems would be installed, but fewer fire exit doors would be required) and zoning code barriers (e.g., allowing parking variances). On the financial side, the water department reduced charges for water and sewer to reflect lower SRO usage, and the housing redevelopment agency arranged low-interest loans to underwrite rents. And, moreover, some of the SROs were given AIA awards for design. Similar efforts are being considered in Atlanta, San Jose, Berkeley, and Richmond. (For more details, see *Planning*, June 1993.)

Promotion of innovative zoning techniques. Innovative site-planning techniques create cost savings by allowing more compact lot sizes and arrangements, more efficient use of infrastructure, and greater densities than are normal under traditional zoning. *Cluster zoning* allows increased densities on a concentrated portion of a development tract. HUD has estimated that the infrastructure costs of a cluster development are 62 percent of those of a conventional development. While most jurisdictions limit cluster standards to PUDs, Dade County, Florida, has successfully employed them as a base district standard. By coupling cluster site plans with a flexible development standard like *zero lot line zoning*, affordable developments can be made aesthetically pleasing with higher open space ratios than those in traditional "cookie-cutter" subdivisions.

Rather than making innovative zoning techniques subject to review, they should be authorized for use as of right by state legislation. New Hampshire, for example, has legislation that prohibits discrimination against cluster proposals.

Integration of inexpensive housing units. Restrictions on the use of manufactured housing and accessory dwelling units must be eliminated or modified. These units are an important part of any strategy to promote affordable housing. Only 16 states currently prohibit discrimination against manufactured housing. New Jersey's Council on Affordable Housing authorizes municipalities to zone for accessory apartments, while California allows local governments to designate areas in residential zones where accessory apartments will be allowed.

Manufactured housing must be allowed in residential districts. Local governments concerned with aesthetics can impose reasonable zoning and site standards that are consistent with those for site-built housing. The use of accessory apartments as a means to meet affordable housing demand should also be allowed. Again, concerns about effects on neighborhood aesthetics and public service delivery can be effectively addressed in local standards for parking, setback, lot coverage, architectural review, and maximum unit size.

Growth management and housing affordability. Many critics of growth management contend that such programs create severe housing affordability problems and are actually new vehicles for exclusionary zoning. To the contrary, a recent study of California growth-control programs found that jurisdictions with strict development controls tended to also have active programs designed to produce low- and moderate-income housing and that jurisdictions *without growth controls* offer no greater share of affordable housing.

In fact, growth management techniques can be used to accommodate affordable housing or to work in a proactive manner to affirmatively promote the construction of such housing. First, the techniques outlined above as reactive measures can be applied (e.g., inclusionary zoning). Furthermore, an *adequate public facilities ordinance (APFO) or concurrency management ordinance* can be designed so that some facility capacity is set aside for affordable housing, thereby preserving land for affordable housing, discouraging speculation, and mitigating the effect of limits on housing supply. Or, if a *development allocation system* is used, it can employ a point system to encourage the production of affordable housing by developers, set aside a specific number of permits for low- and moderate-income housing, or exempt affordable housing from the point system altogether.

A Different Kind of Exaction: The Pimlico Racetrack Impact Fund

This fund was created in 1978 by Maryland's General Assembly to alleviate the negative effects of horse racing on the northwest Baltimore community of Park Heights. For the past 16 years, the state has collected nearly a half-million dollars annually to implement a variety of community programs, ranging from commercial corridor improvements to the development of affordable housing. In 1987, the Northwest Baltimore Development Corporation (NWBDC) was formed to specifically address the deterioration of housing stock in neighborhoods in close proximity of the racetrack. NWBDC was able to use Racetrack Impact Funds as seed capital to hire staff and create a low-interest revolving loan pool to allow area homeowners home improvement loans. NWBDC was also able to build six modular townhouse units and provide subsidies to first-time homebuyers. Currently, NWBDC's plans call for completion of 20 rehabbed units and another 16 to 20 new units. The staff also provides homeownership and credit counseling to neighborhood residents. (Source for this case study was Charles C. Graves, III, Baltimore's Director of City Planning; for more information, contact Marianna Donisi-McCann, Executive Director, NWBDC, 3702 W. Rogers Ave., Baltimore, MD 21215.)

Growth management programs should include specific provisions for the production and maintenance of affordable housing. Accommodations must be made so that regional housing concerns are balanced with local public facilities and environmental issues.

Impact fees and development exactions. Critics contend that impact fees and developer exactions imposed on development are passed along to buyers and renters and, therefore, exacerbate housing affordability problems. Georgia, Florida, Indiana, New Jersey, Arizona, and Vermont currently exempt low- and moderate-income housing from impact fees. Local governments can exempt affordable housing from such fees as long as: any revenue shortfall arising from the exemption is not passed on to market-rate units; the exemption is very specifically targeted to its intended audience; and the developments who benefit from the exemption are subject to ongoing restrictions to ensure that they remain affordable housing.

State legislation should authorize local governments to exempt affordable housing units from impact fees and development exactions.

Environmental legislation and housing affordability. Wetlands legislation has come under extreme fire from developers as being a large contributor to the affordable housing dilemma. While it is true that wetlands and other environmental regulations effectively remove land that might otherwise be eligible for development, the value of the land and the consequences of development on those lands must be measured against the effect on housing availability and affordability within a region (e.g., development in wetlands can result in flooding, groundwater contamination, and loss of recreational areas—all with quantifiable costs). A *transfer of development rights (TDR) program* can be an effective means of protecting environmentally sensitive lands while promoting the higher densities that promote affordable housing.

Environmental regulations should not be and need not be sacrificed to provide for affordable housing. The costs of developing on environmentally sensitive lands are extreme, and environmental damage affects the society as a whole in immeasurable economic and health terms. The effective administration of environmental regulations (e.g., early mapping, time constraints on environmental review) and growth-control techniques like inclusionary zoning and TDRs can counteract the effects of such legislation on housing affordability.

Administrative and procedural reforms. Unanticipated project delays are clearly a major factor affecting housing prices. Delays add to carrying costs and result in investors asking for higher returns, meaning higher housing costs.

Planners must work to alleviate uncertainty and eliminate confusion in the permitting process; abbreviate the approval process; and protect developers investments, thereby alleviating risk. Some of the techniques to achieve these ends are:

- Fixed rather than discretionary standards;
- Permit manuals;
- An ombudsman;
- Time limits for review enforced through use of "deemed approval" provisions;
- One-stop permitting and joint public hearings;
- Increased role of staff in decision making (e.g., administrative approval);
- Development agreements and early vesting;
- Eliminating successive discretionary reviews;
- Establishing that final reviews (such as final plats) are ministerial.

The promotion of certainty in the approval process is of great importance in ensuring the provision of affordable housing. Administrative streamlining, vested rights provisions, the proactive use of development agreements for the specific provision of affordable housing, and the establishment of ongoing public-private partnerships should all be used in the arena of affordable housing so that regulations are not seen as obstructionist and do not, in fact, add to the costs of housing.

THE NEW WAVE: FEDERAL INITIATIVES AND STATE COMPREHENSIVE PROGRAMS

Both state and federal legislation have encouraged innovative housing programs at the local level. The more successful reform efforts involve two major ingredients—a partnership with local governments, allowing housing to assume an appropriate role among the many elements of a comprehensive planning strategy, and funding and authority for effective local implementation, such as state housing trust funds and inclusionary zoning or linkage enabling legislation.

The federal government began this decade recognizing that a new generation of affordable housing initiatives are necessary. Regrettably, the federal legislation has yet to inspire a significant number of innovative local programs. The following paragraphs briefly outline those portions of the Cranston-Gonzalez National Affordable Housing Act of 1990 (NAHA) that hold out promise for a more effective means of providing for housing for low- and moderate-income people.

A Comprehensive Housing Affordability Strategy (CHAS) is required by NAHA if a jurisdiction wants to receive federal assistance under that legislation. The CHAS must include a five-year housing needs assessment; issues and implementation strategies pertaining to homelessness; housing market characteristics; an evaluation of the effect of public policies, such as land-use controls, on housing prices and production; an explanation of the institutional structure of the housing delivery system; a list of funding sources for the purposes of NAHA, including geographic allocation priorities; intergovernmental cooperation strategies; plans for public housing management, including ownership options; and strategies to coordinate use of the Low-Income Housing Tax Credit.

The HOME program, created under NAHA, provides funding for state-local housing production and rehabilitation partnerships. At least 15 percent of HOME Investment Trust Funds must be set aside for non-profit community housing development organizations (CDHOs). Model programs include rental housing production, rental rehabilitation, sweat equity, and second mortgage assistance for first-time homebuyers.

The Low-Income Housing Preservation and Resident Homeownership Act of 1990, Title VI of NAHA, addresses the problem of "expiring uses." More than 350,000 units of federally assisted housing will be withdrawn from the market by their owners in the next 12 years because of expiring mortgages or early payment of those mortgages. The act requires a plan of action that can involve: 1) financial incentives to extend the low-income affordability restrictions; 2) transfer of the units to a qualified purchaser, such as a resident council; and 3) payment of at least one-half of all moving expenses of displaced residents by the project owner.

Other NAHA features still evolving are a National Homeownership Trust, which provides financial assistance to first-time homebuyers, including downpayment assistance and interest-rate buydowns, and the

Homeownership and Opportunity through HOPE Act, which authorizes ownership of public housing units by tenants or other low-income families. The House version of NAHA included two elements that were dropped from the final legislation but that might reappear. Housing opportunity zones (HOZs) are a concept similar to enterprise zones. The House proposal allowed for the federal designation of 50 such zones, where, in return for the "removal" of "regulatory barriers," there would be an increase or preference for federal financial assistance. Connecticut and Maine already have such zones, created by state legislation, but the modification of land-use controls does not appear to play a significant role in their efforts.

Planners need to work closely with local housing departments, housing nonprofits, and community organizations to ensure that planning efforts work in concert with federal programs, especially in ways that enhance opportunities for funding of affordable housing projects.

State Comprehensive Planning for Affordable Housing

Because all local land-use powers are derived from the state through enabling legislation, permanent and lasting initiatives and reforms must be generated at that level. Indeed, as has been noted in the examples offered in this paper, several states have already taken strong action to discourage exclusionary zoning and other cost-inducing regulatory measures. A new generation of programs that balance affordable housing needs with other public policies and objectives, involve sophisticated fair-share planning, and require the use of specific implementation measures to achieve affordability goals and objectives is needed in all states.

States with comprehensive planning legislation have structured their programs to include requirements specifically targeted to promote and provide affordable housing, including:

- The adoption of a local comprehensive plan with a mandatory housing element;
- The establishment of state and/or regional goals, objectives, and policies that bind local governments to the preparation of their comprehensive plans;
- Requirements that all comprehensive planning policies be internally consistent and compatible;

- Requirements that the local comprehensive plan be implemented through the adoption of local land development regulations that are consistent with the plan; and
- The approval of comprehensive plans by a state or regional agency.

Some state legislation also encourages the use of innovative land development regulations (e.g., California promotes inclusionary zoning and linkage policies; Florida encourages inclusionary zoning; Maine suggests the use of cluster zoning, reductions in minimum lot/frontage sizes, and increasing densities; and Washington recommends density bonuses, cluster housing, and planned unit developments as a way to encourage affordable housing).

Mandatory affordable housing planning requirements generally include regional fair-share planning. Some states require the local government to accommodate or produce a fixed number of percentage of affordable dwelling units. Maine requires local governments to achieve a fixed target of 10 percent of new residential development as affordable housing, based on the five-year historical average of residential development within a municipality. Florida, New Jersey, and Washington require that housing elements of the local comprehensive plan include an inventory and analysis of both existing and projected needs, and the designation of adequate sites for low- and moderate-income housing,

---

State Enabling Law Leads to Affordable Housing District

Virginia passed enabling legislation in July 1990 to make it possible for local governments to use comprehensive plans to designate affordable housing areas. Arlington County staff took the opportunity to create an overlay zone that requires developers of high-density projects to protect existing affordable housing or replace it with housing of a comparable type.

For instance, one project in the county for elderly and minority residents, who would otherwise have been displaced, used low-income housing tax credits, a county loan, and density bonuses to create a 103-unit complex (47 new units, 56 rehabilitated units) in which all the units but six are available only to tenants with incomes between 50 and 60 percent of the area's median income. (For further information, call housing development specialist Laurence Newnam, 703-358-3760.)

including multifamily housing, manufactured housing, and subsidized housing. Local governments in Vermont must encourage a diversity of housing types, including a choice between rental and ownership. Vermont also requires plans to support a geographic balance between housing and jobs.

The most far-reaching and innovative legislation has been adopted in California, New Jersey, and Oregon—legislation stimulated, in part, by court orders requiring that local governments accommodate their regional fair share of housing. The New Jersey and California laws were specifically responses to exclusionary zoning litigation and "regional general welfare" mandates of the courts.

New Jersey offers a model for others—statewide comprehensive planning with legislative efforts to implement regional fair-share planning. The state's Council on Affordable Housing (COAH) determines the state's housing regions and local fair-share obligations. Obligations are determined by a complex formula that takes into account a municipality's "present" and "prospective" housing needs, balanced by credits for the accommodation of those needs through new construction or rehabilitation of existing stock. Up to half of a municipality's fair-share obligation may be met through regional agreements with other municipalities.

The law requires that municipalities adopt both a housing element in their comprehensive plan and implementation techniques that provide realistic opportunities for accommodating a fair share of low- and moderate-income housing. Municipalities may request "substantive certification" of the housing element by COAH—certification that creates a presumption of validity in favor of the housing element. Local governments are allowed to phase in their fair-share obligations to accommodate reasonable development priorities and to avoid overtaxing infrastructure capacity. If infrastructure capacity is lacking, new capacity must be reserved for low- and moderate-income projects. The act requires municipalities to consider the following techniques, either alone or in combination, to provide affordable housing:

- Mandatory set-asides or density bonuses;
- Infrastructure expansion;
- Donations of municipally owned land;
- Tax abatements; and

- Targeting of federal/state subsidies.

For inclusionary developments, the COAH regulations require a 20 percent maximum set-aside and a minimum density of six dwelling units per acre. This requirement can be changed only where additional incentives (e.g., increased densities) are offered. Developers can construct these units themselves or pay a fee in lieu of construction. COAH is currently drafting regulations to authorize linkage fees. Restrictive covenants and mortgage liens must be executed by the developer in order to maintain the affordability of these units for a 20-year period.

To support local planning efforts, the state has created a Neighborhood Preservation Nonlapsing Revolving Fund to facilitate planning for jurisdictions with plans that have been certified. These funds may be used for rehabilitation of substandard housing; creation of accessory apartments; conversion on nonresidential space to residential units; acquisition or new construction of housing; technical assistance and site preparation costs; assistance to local housing authority or nonprofits; and infrastructure projects.

All states should adopt comprehensive planning legislation that requires local governments to integrate housing objectives with their overall comprehensive planning framework, including future land use, public facilities and services, environmental protection and conservation, and traffic circulation. This legislation should also create state or regional authorities to determine fair-share obligations for each region and each municipality in a region. State efforts must also provide for funding to implement local affordable housing planning programs.

S. Mark White is an associate attorney with the firm of Freilich, Leitner, Carlisle & Shortlidge, and serves on the board of directors of the Westside Housing Organization in Kansas City, Missouri. Jim Hecimovich is the American Planning Association's Research Manager and Chief Editor of the Planning Advisory Service (PAS) Report series.

2

Transportation, Social Equity, and City-Suburban Connections

By Stephen Cochran, AICP

The rich get rich and the poor get poorer.
popular song
Whiting, Cahn, and Egan, 1921

It seemed clear to us that Cleveland's highest transportation priority should be to ensure a decent level of mobility to those transit dependent persons who were prevented by extreme poverty or a combination of low income and physical disability (including old age) from moving around our metropolitan area.
Norman Krumholz,
Journal of the American Planning Association
Spring 1982

In 1968, the Kerner Commission proposed the "spacial mismatch hypothesis" as one cause of urban poverty and unrest: both manufacturing and service jobs requiring relatively lower educational attainment are moving to the suburbs; those with lower educational levels are disproportionately located in the center cities and are particularly affected by the move of such jobs; central-city residents lack access to the jobs that have moved, due to inadequate transportation or to the inability to relocate their residences closer to the moved jobs; central-city residents lack the education and skills to fill the new, higher-skilled service-sector jobs being created in central cities.

The years since the Kerner Commission have strengthened this hypothesis. While the 1980s created millions of new jobs, 80 percent of them were outside of central cities (Covington 1993). More than 60 percent of all office space in the U.S. is now in suburbs or exurbs (USDOT Federal Highway Administration 1992). Manufacturing and lower-level service jobs are locating at the outermost rings of urban growth (or in central America, southeast Asia, and eastern Europe). Before the '89-'92 recession, the labor pool in the outer suburbs could not keep up with job growth, and employers experienced severe labor shortages despite a surplus of potential workers in the central cities.

Meanwhile, downtown and inner-ring job growth has been almost exclusively in white collar or higher-skilled clerical positions. As the skills required for city jobs have increased, the percentage of city residents completing high school has declined and general education achievement has slightly declined.

Billions of dollars have been poured into highways that have opened up the countryside to those with automobiles and into mass transit aimed at stabilizing central business districts by ensuring convenient, subsidized access to the central business district. Transportation programs consciously aimed at connecting inner-city residents with lower-skilled suburban jobs have remained marginal and funded at levels in the millions, not billions of dollars. Such city-to-suburbs programs are still viewed by researchers and transportation planners as experimental, innovative, and not yet proven on a large scale, although they have been tried since the early '70s. Yet, twice as many Hispanic households, and three times as many African-American households did not own an automobile in 1980 as was the case for white households (Fox 1992).

Transportation policies of the last 60 years did much to bring about this "spacial mismatch." Today's decentralized urban regions are not conceivable without the emphasis the federal and state governments have given to funding highways rather than transit. These transportation policies have combined with mortgage subsidies, land use, tax and energy policies, new technologies, anti-urban impulses, and racism to make widely spread metropolitan regions the standard development form.

Given the strength of the new urban pattern it is unlikely that what transportation hath wrought, transportation can, by itself, undo. Social equity solutions are far more likely to be found in changing land-use patterns, tax structures, housing policies, and education and job-training systems.

APA OBJECTIVES FOR EQUITY IN TRANSPORTATION POLICIES

APA adopted eight policies on transportation in 1990. The transportation/equity policy states:

> Transportation policies should ensure mobility for the aged, the disadvantaged, the young, the handicapped, and other transportation disadvantaged people, whether urban or rural. Plans and policies should be selected only after assessing the impacts of user fees and other financing on the ability-to-pay of those affected. Where adverse equity impacts are likely, compensating actions may be taken in the form of income transfers, transportation service alternatives, and temporary transitional subsidies.

As part of APA's work on an agenda to increase social equity in America's communities, this paper looks at issues of transportation planning and social equity, particularly with respect to ensuring access to work for the economically disadvantaged in urban areas.

It outlines traditional transportation policies and practices, explores innovations that may help improve transportation and social equity, and recommends actions planners can take to use transportation as a tool for enhancing social equity.

TRADITIONAL TRANSPORTATION POLICIES AND PRACTICES

Traditional Transportation Planning Philosophy. Transportation planners have aimed to speed the movement of vehicles by relieving congestion. Transportation planning and construction has aimed to increase capacity, usually by building more highway lanes. Occasionally, demand reduction has been considered, but usually in the context of reducing demand on one mode by increasing the capacity on another parallel mode. Until fairly recently, transportation planning has focused on movement of goods and trips to work, not the overall relation between transportation and quality of life.

General Modal Patterns. Transportation planning in urban areas aimed, first, at "opening up" dense central cities with parkways and interstates to give the middle-class access to less dense, greener, and more "protected" residential environments. Until World War II, the centripetal policies were at least partially balanced in well-established cities by the expansion of radial transit lines connecting the suburbs and central cities. From the mid-'30s until the late 1960s, almost all transportation policy and construction focused on highway construction and keeping up with post-war decentralization. Transit planning and construction began again in the 1960s.

Financing Patterns. Government expenditures have usually favored highways over other modes, such as rail and transit. The pattern started early. In the heyday of the railroads, government participation rarely ventured beyond land writedowns or gifts. Transit systems in older American cities were built as private concerns.

Highways were different. Aside from private 19th century turnpikes and a few private toll roads for which planning began in the 1980s, major road building generally has been a governmental responsibility. As early as four years after the first Model T, the U.S. and state governments had embarked on a taxpayer funded national highway system. This participation peaked with the interstate highway system, 90 percent funded by the federal government. Transit systems, however, were built without federal participation until the 1970s, when some systems received 80 percent funding from the federal government. Federal participation in the 1980s was generally 70 percent for non-interstate federally designated roads and 60 percent for mass transit systems.

Significantly, the Intermodal Surface Transportation Efficiency Act of 1991 (ISTEA) is more "modal neutral" than previous transportation acts and lets modal decisions be made at the state and local levels. It equalizes federal funding for most highway and transit construction at 80 percent.

INEQUITIES IN TRANSPORTATION POLICIES AND CONSTRUCTION

Radial highways made suburban living possible for those who could afford a car and house. Circumferential roads made possible the development of suburban employment centers that were accessible without travelling though central cities. The radial commuting patterns, which were well-served by transit, were supplemented and eventually surpassed by non-radial patterns that could not be served by traditional transit. For various reasons, housing affordable to less-educated and less-skilled workers did not follow similar jobs to the suburbs. Without adequate affordable housing in the suburbs, even developing "Edge City" patterns (i.e., suburban and exurban "downtowns) will not alleviate this disconnection. Living far from the new jobs, central-city residents need transportation to jobs that is least as efficient as that used by suburbanites.

Traditional transportation planning has not designed such systems. Federal funding formulas favored highway construction. The politics of transit planning and construction favored expensive new fixed rail systems serving suburban commuters, rather than cheaper, more flexible bus or paratransit systems that could be adapted to serving the "reverse commute" needs of inner-city residents going to suburban jobs, and the nonradial needs of suburb-to-suburb commuters.

Where new rapid transit systems were created, their orientation was toward maintaining central-city accessibility for suburban commuters or maintaining a "no net increase" of cars entering the old downtowns. Where new transit systems were planned with adequate coverage in disadvantaged neighborhoods, the politics of financing and ridership marketing favored building lines serving the wealthier transit riders first. The patterns continue. Washington, D.C., has opened only small portions of the subway line serving the neighborhoods most impacted by the riots of the late '60s; the line connecting the second wealthiest county in the country with downtown Washington was 80 percent complete 10 years ago. Cleveland is spending over $600 million on a six-mile rail line serving the wealthiest four percent of Cleveland's transit riders, while 87 percent of the city's transit ridership depends on buses (Krumholz 1991).

The new rail system in Los Angeles has developed innovative approaches to increasing service provided to economically impacted communities. Still, community-oriented planners continue to question the wisdom of the basic rail system itself (Grigsby 1992). In cities as varied as Buffalo, Detroit, and Miami, ridership on new transit systems is far below projections. While the federal government picked up the tab for most of the construction costs for these systems, it is the local governments that must pay the annual operating subsidies, often to the detriment of more humble transit forms serving less advantaged riders.

It has become increasingly difficult for minorities and lower-skilled workers to get to suitable new jobs without an automobile. And, in Catch-22 fashion, it has also become difficult to afford to buy an automobile without access to the jobs for which the automobile was needed.

The impact of the freeways that changed these land uses and commuting patterns was not limited to longer-term effects, such as housing and job dispersal. They had very direct and immediate negative impacts on the disadvantaged residents of cities. When freeways could not be located in floodplains, along rail lines, or in parks, they were usually sited through areas offering the least political resistance (i.e., disadvantaged neighborhoods with less clout). Inner-city jobs were displaced, although they may have left eventually anyway as part of the general spatial restructuring of the economy. Residents were displaced, destroying neighborhoods and disrupting the family, social, and institutional ties of those citizens with the fewest resources for re-establishing those ties.

It was not until the early 1970s that national environmental, historic preservation, and citizen participation requirements provided the legal tools to slow the construction of freeways and begin to force some balance of expenditures among transportation modes.

In a number of ways, then, the transportation policies of the last half century have contributed to the decline of central cities and the quality of life of central-city residents.

INNOVATIVE TRANSPORTATION PLANNING POLICIES AND PRACTICES

ISTEA, which was crafted with substantial participation by the American Planning Association and other pro-planning groups, emphasizes connections among transportation modes and the connection of transportation to quality of life. It requires both planning and program funds to be used to make some of these connections.

ISTEA and Social Equity . . .

Sections 134(f) and 135(c) of ISTEA require metropolitan planning organizations (MPOs) and state departments of transportation to consider "the overall social, economic, energy and environmental effects of transportation decisions . . . and the . . . effect of transportation decisions on land use and development [and] consistency [between] transportation [and] the provisions of all applicable short-range and long-range land use and development plans." MPOs must also consider "methods to expand and enhance transit services and to increase the use of such services."

These planning requirements, combined with more modal-neutral financing formulas begin to level the playing field between transit and highways. More importantly for planners, they acknowledge that the relationship between a community's *desired* land use and future transportation construction and programs must be considered. ISTEA encourages communities to look at transportation in the context of the community's vision of its overall quality of life.

More than most other groups, planners have understood the comprehensive nature of the spacial mismatch problem. They have advocated changes in policy and practice that would address the issue through more comprehensive transportation planning policies and through more rational land uses. Through support of mixed-use zoning and inclusionary housing practices in the suburbs, and through neighborhood development programs and empowerment zones in the cities, planners have sought to bring disadvantaged residents closer to the jobs for which their educational levels and training are most suitable.

There are transportation planning tools that have helped address the problem, but they usually work best when used in combination with other planning tools and human resources programs. The most enlightened transportation policies will have only marginal effects unless combined with a comprehensive approach to the problem. Better schools, job training, personal responsibility coaching, day care, job and transportation marketing, and concerted efforts to overcome racial stereotyping are essential.

An outline of innovative transportation planning tools follows. They are grouped into five categories:

    A.   Enhancing Physical Connections Between Inner-City Residents and Suburban Jobs

    B.   Financial Incentives to Promote Transit

    C.   Transportation Construction as an Income Generator

    D.   Transportation and Land-Use Tools to Promote Equity

    E.   Regulatory and Governmental Changes

Enhancing Physical Connections Between Inner-City Residents and Suburban Jobs

In 1980, over 30 percent of African-American households lacked access to an automobile (Fox 1992). This makes some form of improved transit or paratransit the most realistic option for improving connections to jobs. Many of the basic facilities for such transit are already in place. But most operational patterns favor commuting from the suburbs to the central city, not the "reverse commute" from the city to the suburbs. What is needed most is to change thinking about feeder and distribution systems, and pricing mechanisms to make reverse commuting and dispersed commuting as feasible as traditional radial commuting from suburbs to the central city.

Additional public transit. In metropolitan areas with relatively high densities it may be feasible to provide reverse-commute service through traditional transit systems. Planning studies, facilities construction and capital purchases are eligible for funding under Title III of ISTEA.

The financing dynamics, and need for such lines will, of course, change in weaker economic times. But the potential for such service remains great in areas with commuter rail or heavy rail, major employment nodes, and corridors. Planners can take the lead in identifying potential areas, initiate feasibility surveys with developers and employers, and study the implications of having commuter trains provide reverse commute service, rather than "deadheading" (i.e., stopping the run at the terminus of a traditional commute pattern, and waiting for the return trip at the other end of the commute cycle).

There is some evidence that sustaining such reverse commute service may be difficult. Journey to work time in reverse commute situations dramatically favors the automobile. A heavily used reverse commute route in the Washington, D.C., area takes 20 minutes by auto and 59 minutes by transit (Washington Metropolitan Council of Governments [WashCOG] 1991). A similar study in Baltimore found the same one-to-three ratio of car-trip to transit-trip time (Farkas 1990, 79). Where direct multiple collection and distribution point service had been provided by the Washington transportation authority, ridership was heavy during the first two years, and dropped off significantly after that. Surveys found that the majority of "lapsed" riders had used their newly higher incomes to purchase a car and reduce their commuting time (WashCOG 1991; similarly, Regional Plan Association 1972). While such increases in low-income purchasing power and mobility might be considered social equity "successes," the switch from transit to automobile may be considered a setback for some of transportation planning's environmental and congestion-reduction objectives.

Paratransit options. Where publicly provided reverse commute transit may not be feasible, a variety of public, private, or joint paratransit options may be able to provide more successful and flexible service. There are limits on their eligibility for ISTEA funding.

Employer-provided distribution networks. There are numerous examples of major employers providing regular shuttle service from transit stops to employment centers or pooling their efforts in Transportation Management Associations (TMAs). In Fairfax County, Virginia, for example, the Mobil Corporation offers free shuttle service during rush hours from the Washington area Metrorail station to the company's headquarters. Some employers have even provided direct service from central-city pick-up centers to suburban employment nodes. However, information seems to be anecdotal. There is a need for hard research on the parameters of ridership levels, land-use densities, numbers of transfers and commute times that make for successful service. With such figures, planners could work directly with the private sector to promote such service where suitable.

Entrepreneurial programs. The Federal Transit Administration's Entrepreneurial Services Program was started in 1987 to spur private-sector

The SEPTA Success Story

The Philadelphia area's Southeastern Pennsylvania Transportation Authority (SEPTA) "200 Series" feeder bus routes heavily involve employers and transportation management associations (TMAs) in linking suburban rail stations with four large industrial and office parks and a regional shopping mall. The first route was initiated by a major office park developer whose tenants were experiencing labor shortages during the '80s boom. This line proved profitable enough that promised operating subsidizes from developers and employers were unnecessary and the profit was used to subsidize the reverse-direction commuter rail service feeding the bus line. Of the four other lines that have been started, one has been profitable and the four lines' overall operating ratio of 90 percent is very favorable. The flexibility of buses has also allowed the adjustment of lines in reaction to regional economic slowdowns. Four percent of all SEPTA riders are reverse commuters (Wartzman 1993; Bickel 1993).

initiatives in transportation. With 58 percent of commuting trips being from suburb to suburb in 1980, and the trend having accelerated in the last 12 years, FTA has provided incentives for private experimentation in commuter service not traditionally provided by the public sector. It subsidizes start-up programs for two years. Interestingly, of the 59 programs funded by 1989, 29 were for small private operators who initiated reverse commute services not from suburb to suburb, but between inner-city neighborhoods and suburban job sites (Hughes 1989). Being entrepreneurially based, the services can provide flexible response to changing employer and employee needs. Providers have been as varied as a public housing management corporation in Chicago that convinced employers to support running city-to-suburb vans and a private transportation supplier in Texas under contract to transport Aid to Families with Dependent Children (AFDC) recipients participating in job-training programs.

Planners can assist such services by providing basic census and market data and by incorporating listings of entrepreneurial services in comprehensive transit listings and schedules.

Van pooling and ride sharing. Private individuals have always had informal car-pooling networks. After the oil price shocks of the '70s, these became more formalized, with large private employers and government agencies providing coordinating services for their employees. In many areas that do not meet Environmental Protection Agency standards for air quality, governments have mandated such services for large private and public employers. However, publicly coordinated sharing of information among such employers has proved to be cumbersome. To reduce air pollution and congestion, Title I of ISTEA allows the construction of new high occupancy vehicle (HOV) lanes, thus encouraging van-pooling and ride sharing. Van-pooling and ride-sharing programs are eligible for funding under the Surface Transportation Program of ISTEA. They are likely to become increasingly important for those already employed, but they do not seem particularly useful for those not yet employed in jobs served by such services. Transportation planners may wish to explore computerized "on-line" hook-ups between those providing vans and rides and the social welfare agencies seeking transportation for their clients. However, the insurance, liability, and social problems such matches would likely encounter seem to make this alternative somewhat unattractive. Employer-provided or publicly provided transit subsidies could not be used for unincorporated "pool" organizers or drivers.

Community-based and other nonprofit services. The newest innovation in paratransit is to initiate planning from the community end. Resident management groups or nonprofit human resource development groups have incorporated the provision of transportation to jobs into their comprehensive approach to empowerment and quality-of-life improvement.

Large public or publicly assisted housing developments, or community development corporations, operate fleets of vans to transport residents to transit lines or directly to major employers. As part of their regular job-training programs, they also provide counseling on how to understand transit schedules, the importance of promptness and timetables, etc.

Such services require public subsidies, and these come from a broad array of sources, including housing, employment, social services, and transportation programs at the local, state, regional, and national levels, some of which may be eligible for funding under ISTEA.

Financial Incentives to Promote Transit

Reduce reverse commute fares. Some transit systems increase fares during rush hours. While the literature is full of suggestions that reducing reverse commute fares to non-rush-hour prices would reduce the cost of commuting of central-city residents, it is an idea more promised than practiced.

An alternative is expansion of transit subsidies for central-city residents and those less able to afford transit through provision of transit passes. Employers can provide passes worth up to $60 a month without their being considered taxable income. Governments can provide passes under a number of social programs, but not through ISTEA.

Bring about parity between the ceiling for tax-free transit subsidies and the floor for taxable employer-provided parking. As indicated above, employer-provided transit subsidies greater than $60 per month are taxed as regular income. Employees do not have to pay taxes on employer-provided parking benefits until they are equivalent to $155 a month. Planners should consider making efforts to support changes to treat each mode comparably in this respect by increasing the tax-exempt transit subsidies to the level of tax-free parking subsidies.

Study the implications of decreasing indirect public subsidies for the private automobile. Depending on the externalities considered in the study, the average automobile driver is calculated to pay between 82 and 89 percent of the estimated total of direct and indirect public,

---

ISTEA's Enhancement Provisions

ISTEA's Title I "enhancement" provisions 10 percent of all Surface Transportation Program funds must be reserved for enhancements such as day care centers, bike trails, etc. Rehabilitation or conversion of some aging transportation facilities may serve as catalysts for economic development or community enhancement. An obsolete railroad station, for instance, may be able to be converted with ISTEA funds into a community center or the nucleus for a new shopping facility. This would generate both construction-related and permanent jobs.

private, and social costs for every auto mile driven (Konheim and Ketchum 1993; Moore and Thorsnes 1994). Whatever figure is accepted, the public subsidy for automobile travel is considerable. Proposals to increase gasoline taxes and fuel efficiency standards, initiate congestion pricing on highway and bridge facilities, and expand the use of toll roads are aimed at moving public policy towards reflecting the real cost to the public of automobile usage and to motivating shifts to transportation modes other than the automobile. However, unless such cost increases are mitigated through income transfers, they may have a disproportionate cost on the disadvantaged (*Governing* 1993).

The National Urban League regularly questions whether such environmentally sound policies might not be regressive social policies (Tidwell 1991). As long as the use of automobiles by central-city minority groups remains close to its current level of one-half that of white suburbanites, the regressive impact will not be as great as the Urban League fears. However, since it is unlikely that even the most progressive public transportation policies will be able to keep up with increasing decentralization trends, automobile usage will probably become a more important option for access to jobs and shopping for those central-city residents that can afford automobiles. It is possible that if innovative transit and paratransit options prove infeasible to implement on a widespread basis, subsidizing the purchase and operation (e.g., insurance) of private automobiles by the disadvantaged may prove to be an alternative worth examining from a social equity standpoint.

Transportation-Related Construction as an Income Generator for Central-City Residents

The National Urban League's Urban Marshall Plan is based on the assumption that the best solution to poverty is jobs. The league emphasizes transportation and infrastructure construction jobs as providers of immediate jobs and of improved potential for future economic and job growth.

According to the league, highways generate 22,000 jobs per billion dollars expended, and transit provides 1,800 full-time jobs for every $20 million invested in improvements and operations (Tidwell 1991). The league is more bullish on highways than on transit, because jobs tend to come on-line sooner and because the league understandably wants to move center-city residents into the mainstream of auto mobility.

Planners need to work with regional authorities to ensure a balanced mix of construction projects that will move traffic and goods, ensure mobility (especially access to jobs for all groups), promote modal options for all groups, and minimize environmental impacts.

As a profession dedicated to promoting equity, it will likely fall to planners to help promote voluntary employment and training agreements that ensure a fair share of employment and training for minorities and center-city residents in transportation construction and maintenance. It would be helpful to survey local and regional transportation authorities for model employment and training agreements and ensure their availability to all transportation planners.

Transportation and Land Use Tools to Promote Equity

Breaking the Spatial Mismatch. Reducing the need for long commutes by the less-advantaged or less-abled residents of a metropolitan area would help reduce their transit dependency. This could be accomplished by:

- bringing affordable housing closer to less skilled jobs;
- reducing discrimination in renting and home financing;
- bringing less-skilled jobs closer to those most in need of such jobs, and vice-versa;
- improving the skills and marketability of central-city residents;
- reducing physical space distinctions through telecommuting.

Some of these approaches are covered in more detail in other agenda papers. Linkages and exactions promote affordable housing in suburban areas. Studies in several metropolitan areas, particularly the San Francisco Bay Area, show that closer proximity of affordable housing and jobs reduces commuting times, although job/home proximity is not the only factor determining housing choice. Empowerment zones may retain some lesser-skilled jobs in central cities, or even bring a few back in.

In the transportation area, planners are teaming up with human resource and job specialists to explore the advantages of expanded telecommuting as a way of bringing lower-skilled back-office jobs back to central cities.

Establish social support and convenience facilities close to transit stations. Getting to and from day care, the dry cleaners and the convenience store is part of the trip to work. With transit-dependent, inner-city, reverse-commute residents already spending two to three times as long on their commute as auto drivers, consolidating work-related side trips is particularly important. San Francisco's Bay Area transit system, for example, has already constructed prototype day-care centers at BART transit stops and transfer points. Although these were initiated before the passage of ISTEA, such facilities would now be eligible for ISTEA funding as "enhancements."

Require more mixed-use zoning at suburban employment centers. Mixed uses are needed at the job site, too. Transit-dependent workers need basic retail services in close proximity to jobs, to be able to walk to them over lunch. The suburban office park norm assumes workers that do not eat in the employee cafeteria will drive to lunch and will "run errands" at auto-oriented development on the way to or from work. This may not be an option for transit-dependent workers.

Update design standards to make suburban commercial centers more accessible to non-automobile users. Current suburban roadway, access,

---

Telecommuting Centers in LA:
The Potential for Improving Access to Jobs

In Los Angeles, even before the 1994 earthquake made telecommuting an imperative for some people, air-quality non-attainment problems were already prompting an aggressive look at telecommuting. To comply with air-quality district requirements, the city and county are establishing telecommuting centers in several parts of the city. Just as community development agencies provided pooled services for some start-up small businesses in the '80s, so Los Angeles in the '90s will provide facilities for back-office telecommuting functions to reduce commuting trips. These are the very types of jobs that had been moving to outer suburbs in the '80s to reduce office space costs (and, some have contended, to get away from people of color). If coupled with aggressive skills-training, the spin-off advantage of telecommuting for social equity is the possibility of moving lower-level clerical jobs closer to lower-skilled residents. The Los Angeles experience should be monitored closely by planners and results shared throughout the planning network.

and setback standards assume auto arrival as the primary means of access. Planners should revise design standards to make both building sating and actual buildings more accessible, more "friendly" and safer for pedestrians, cyclists, and transit users. ISTEA's enhancement provisions can help fund such changes for bikeways, sidewalks, etc.

Integrate transit schedules and information about schedules. Reducing transfer time and letting potential riders know schedules can decrease commuting time for the transit-dependent and increase overall ridership.

Change land uses at transit stations and stops. Commercial development at stops, or within a 10-minute walk, can generate jobs not completely dependent on automobile usage. Planners can promote higher-density Transit Oriented Development for reverse commuters rather than, or in addition to, surface parking for commuters transferring to inbound transit.

Reexamine assumptions about the superiority of rail transit over bus transit. While greater densities may be a desirable long-range objective, planners may need to take a much harder, more objective look at the assumed superiority of rail transit over bus transit. A quick literature search indicates that planners share a romance for the rails that may not be conducive to promoting transit options that give the most service to the most transit-dependent populations.

Unless planned rail transit is coupled with firm, legally binding commitments by governments to increase zoning densities and the mix of uses, the operating subsidies for future rail transit may drain resources from improving the humbler transit modes that can serve central-city residents now. And unless rail transit is coupled with flexible central-city collection/suburban distribution systems, the rail transit may do little to help the transit-dependent in the future.

Under ISTEA, metropolitan Transportation Improvement Plans (TIPs) and State Implementation Plans (SIPs) must give greater consideration to financial constraints than in the past. Proposed choices must be shown to have a realistic chance of being financed. This may encourage harder looks at "humbler" solutions.

Avoid being dogmatic about the desired physical end state. Planners tend to be strong supporters of relatively dense settlement patterns with a strong central focus, and the transit that such patterns can support. We champion the rebuilding of older communities and creation of new jobs in them.

Many central-city residents would just as soon leave for the suburbs and don't care where their jobs are as long as they can get to them (Lawman 1994). For social equity purposes, increased mobility for poorer citizens may be just as important for planners to foster as more environmentally sound and transit-accessible land-use patterns.

Regulatory and Governmental Changes

Stronger regional planning and regional government authorities. Existing governmental structures are poorly equipped to meet social equity goals through transportation. Metropolitan transportation authorities can approve transit location, type, and frequency but cannot establish related zoning requirements or land-use plans. Similarly, suburban governments can legislate exclusionary zoning or discriminatory transportation networks, while state or city governments are unable to respond effectively. Sections 134 and 135 of ISTEA require TIPs and SIPs to be coordinated among jurisdictions and their transportation and land-use plans, but they stop far short of forcing metropolitanwide government.

Planners should champion the stronger role envisioned for Metropolitan Planning Organizations under ISTEA. Section 134 emphasizes MPOs' needs to coordinate transportation, land use, and social equity issues.

Such advocacy may meet with opposition from central-city governments as a dilution of hard-won minority power in a majority-dominated region. Planners will need to tactfully point out that greater control of the relatively few financial resources remaining in central cities may be less desirable for central-city residents and central-city futures than shared control of the far greater stock of financial resources at the regional level.

Include social equity considerations in any adequate facilities standards. Progressive jurisdictions require that "adequate facilities" be in place before new commercial or residential developments come on line. Such facilities are usually defined to be water, sewer, waste treatment, schools, and roads. Planners should examine the feasibility of developing adequate facilities standards that would include transportation connections to low-skilled employee bases or to high unemployment areas as one of the "facilities" that had to be in place for project approval. Ideally, the connections would be interjurisdictional. The legal implications of expanding the definition of facilities to include such connections would have to be thoroughly examined first.

Increase involvement in the legislative and regulatory arena. ISTEA promises to give transportation planners and providers greater flexibility in choosing and financing transportation options most appropriate to different users or geographical situations. It is important that planners at all levels maintain involvement with the legislative and regulatory process for implementing ISTEA as regulations develop.

Planners may want to consider advocating federal legislation that would give social equity the same procedural and legal status now enjoyed by environmental and historic resources under the National Environmental Policy Act and Section 106 of the Federal Highway Act. The "lawsuit power" of such legislation could put such concerns on more equal footing with economic development and mobility.

Increase citizen participation modality and transportation improvement choices. ISTEA promotes flexibility and choice through broad-based citizen participation in the TIP. Public hearings help plans achieve formal political legitimacy and are great for hearing what should *not* be built. They are generally not as good at building support and uncovering community-based innovative ideas for solving transportation needs. Participation is often skewed to the people who have the skills and the time to participate in the process. These are not the characteristics of socially disadvantaged transportation user groups.

While Sections 134 and 135 of ISTEA are new, planners should work to establish a tradition of encouraging focus groups, community-based visioning processes and other innovative citizen participation methods described elsewhere in the agenda papers as a part of the TIP and SIP process. Planners should help low-income transportation users be aware of their rights to advocate their own solutions to their perceived needs and to fight projects they determine to have an adverse affect on their communities. *All* communities have the right to participate in the setting of priorities and modal choices under ISTEA.

SUMMARY RECOMMENDATIONS

While ISTEA does not give "lawsuit power" to social equity impacts, it does acknowledge the need to consider social impacts and the relationships among a community's desired quality of life, land uses and transportation facilities. It gives communities and states considerable flexibility in transportation planning and for spending transportation dollars. Planners need to use these ISTEA provisions to give social equity considerations far greater weight than in the past when considering transportation policies and projects. This will be difficult to achieve for many reasons. There is a mismatch between the regional economic development scale driving most transportation decisions and the small-scale, neighborhood development context at which low-income job creation and job-matching efforts are focused. Planners need to remember that transportation should connect people—all groups of people—with opportunities, not just one geographic area with another.

A broad range of planners can get involved in promoting transportation decisions that enhance social equity. There are opportunities for traditionally trained transportation planners to make better physical connections between inner-city residents and suburban jobs. Economic development and financial planners can refine financial incentives for better transit. Capital improvement planners can help generate transportation construction and spin-off jobs aiding inner-city residents. Land-use planners, zoning administrators, and urban designers can develop new land-use, zoning, and building standards that make developments more accessible to the disadvantaged. All planners can promote innovative regulations and stress the connections between city and suburbs in regional governing deliberations.

In many instances, there are opportunities for planners to take the lead in research, development, and circulation of successful models, community outreach, and legislative advocacy. But, at all levels, planners need to stop thinking of transportation planning as something to relieve traffic congestion in the suburbs and start thinking of it as a tool for reestablishing connections in our urban regions, until they are once again whole.

SELECTED LIST OF SOURCES AND REFERENCES

Bristol, Robert. "Philadelphia Links Bus and Rail." *Planning,* December 1993, 21, 22.

Center for Neighborhood Technology & Martinez and Associates. "Reverse Commuting on the Metra Milwaukee District/West Line: A Feasibility Study." June 4, 1990.

Covington, Mary Rose. "Intermodalism at Work: Presentation to Congressional Black Caucus Transportation Brain Trust." Greater Cleveland Regional Transit Authority. Sept. 17, 1993.

Farkas, Z. Andrew, Abiodun Odunmbaku, and Moges Ayele. *Low-Wage Labor and Access to Suburban Jobs.* USDOT/UMTA. January, 1990.

Fox, Charles J. *Environmental and Social Justice Priorities in Transportation.* Human Environment Center. Washington, D.C. 1992.

Governing. "Congestion Pricing: Going Somewhere Slowly." October 1993, 49-52.

Grigsby, J. Eugene III. Presentation to the Assembly Special Committee on the Los Angeles Crisis: Urban Planning and Transit. July 24, 1992.

Hughes, Mark Alan. "Employment Decentralization and Accessibility: A Strategy for Stimulating Regional Mobility." *Journal of the American Planning Association* (Summer 1991).

_____. *Fighting Poverty in Cities: Transportation Programs as Bridges to Opportunity.* Research Report of the National League of Cities. 1989.

_____. *Poverty in Cities.* Research Report of the National League of Cities. 1989.

Klein, Robert J. "Access to Jobs A Public Transit Agency's Initiative for Privately Operated Service." Transportation Research Record 1349 (1993): 120.

Konheim and Ketchum, Inc. "Costs of Roadway Transportation Nationally, for Central City, Suburban and Non-Metropolitan Area." January 6, 1993.

Krumholz, Norman. "Equity and Local Economic Development." *Economic Development Quarterly* 5, no. 4 (November 1991): 297.

Lemann, Nicholas. "The Myth of Community Development." *NY Times Magazine,* January 9, 1994.

Los Angeles County Transportation Commission. Nickerson Gardens TDM Project. 1992.

Metropolitan Washington Council of Governments, National Capital Regional Transportation Board. *The Region* 32, no. 2 (December 1991).

Moore, Terry, and Paul Thorsnes. "The Transportation/Land Use Connection." Planning Advisory Service Report No. 448/449. Chicago: American Planning Association, January 1994.

Nelson, Toya. "Wisconsin Picks Up the Tab." *Planning,* December 1993, 18, 19.

Tidwell, Billy J. "Playing to Win: A Marshall Plan for America." National Urban League. July 1991.

USDOT/FHWA. "Edge City and ISTEA—Examining the Transportation Implications of Suburban Development Patterns." *Searching for Solutions.* Number 7. December 1992.

USDOT. Intermodal Surface Transportation Efficiency Act of 1991. U.S. Government Printing Office. 1991.

Wartzman, Rick . "New Bus Lines Link the Inner-City Poor With Jobs in Suburbia." *Wall Street Journal,* September 24, 1993, A1, A4.

Williams, Kristine M. "ISTEA: New Directions for Transportation." *Land Use Law & Zoning Digest,* July 1993.

Wolter, Patti. "Reverse Commute Links City Workers, Suburban Jobs." *The Neighborhood Works,* October-November 1990, 11-12.

Stephen Cochran is the Director for Council Programs at the American Planning Association.

3

Environmental LULUs:
Is There an Equitable Solution?

By Jim Schwab

The issue of locally unwanted land uses (LULUs) has often been a policy maker's nightmare. Siting a facility whose social benefits are diffuse and whose negative impacts are concentrated on an unfortunate few can be a highly unpopular task. Yet the issue can also be a policy maker's opportunity, but only if it is first perceived as fundamentally a philosophical issue that must be transformed, whenever possible, into a win-win scenario rather than a win-lose scenario.

And, in that sense, the acronym itself may be a disservice to planning professionals. Each word in the phrase and the resulting acronym itself are laden with value judgments. "Locally," for instance, immediately conjures up the images behind another acronym—NIMBY, or "not in my backyard." Is the so-called LULU unwanted locally, or is the facility, in fact, generally undesirable or perhaps merely unnecessary? If public policy analysis has skipped or glided over that question, it is already on a collision course with public perceptions. "Unwanted" raises the obvious question, by whom? And if a facility is "locally unwanted," it is by definition wanted by someone else somewhere else, or it would not even be on the public agenda. If it is to be a "land use," of course, it must be put somewhere, presuming the original decision that it must be put somewhere at all. Finally, the resulting acronym, LULU, sardonically suggests an issue that is bound to raise hackles. Just think of the other contexts in which we use the word *lulu*. Webster's (labeling it slang) defines it as "one that is remarkable or wonderful." Indeed.

There is even more at issue. The phrase has tended to muddle some issues by its inclusivity, taking in both issues of social LULUs, such as group homes, public housing projects, and AIDS hospices, and environmental LULUs, such as nuclear power plants, airports, and hazardous waste treatment, storage, and disposal facilities. There is almost no evidence, however, that the same people react to both types of facilities in the same ways and for the same reasons. Nor is it always clear that all the environmental LULUs are as vital to society's general welfare as the social LULUs. Social LULUs have historically been driven by civil rights concerns, such as racial and religious discrimination, handicapped access, and the need for decent housing for low-income citizens. Environmental LULUs are driven largely by technological change and the expanding effluvia of a prosperous industrial society. They raise far

---

Landfill in the Sky?

"A landfill in the sky" is how some East Liverpool, Ohio, residents contemptuously refer to the controversial WTI hazardous-waste incinerator located on the banks of the Ohio River. The small industrial town (pop. 17,000) once was the "pottery capital of the world," capitalizing on its abundant clay supplies, then hosted a major steel plant until it shut down in the 1970s. Double-digit unemployment followed, accompanied by a mayor's desire to find new industry and new jobs. When WTI offered to locate its facility in East Liverpool, it seemed like a godsend—until inquiring residents pored through the technical reports to learn what environmental threats were in the bargain. Among them: The plant, located at the bottom of a ravine in this steeply terraced river town, would sit just 300 feet from the nearest residential housing in a low-income neighborhood, and just 1,100 feet from the elementary school that serves the area. Moreover, the plant is in the heart of a river valley famous in meteorological literature for its air inversions, in which stagnant, polluted air can become trapped by a higher warm-air mass and linger for days or weeks. Mayor John Payne, who had welcomed WTI, lost his job in the ensuing uproar. Businesses that had supported WTI's arrival often became the objects of consumer boycotts.

When construction finally began in the fall of 1990 after protracted legal battles, environmental opposition exploded, leading to contentious, and in some cases canceled, public hearings, civil disobedience actions against the plant in which the protesters were acquitted, and a town so bitterly divided that it may take years for the wounds to heal. Instead of becoming a symbol of East Liverpool's resurgence, WTI has instead become the focus of its intense soul-searching.

more questions about the equitable distribution of the risks and benefits of industrial progress. The increased opposition of civil rights and labor organizations to what they perceive as the inequitable burden of environmental LULUs is vivid testimony to the fact that the issues are not identical. These very people supported most of the civil rights agenda that mandated equitable land-use considerations for the social LULUs. In other words, they see it as entirely consistent to separate these two issues and advocate on opposite sides of the fence. It is erroneous to ascribe the same motives to all LULU opposition because the identity of motive simply does not exist.

Whose Backyard?

There is, of course, always some overlap, but it is seldom significant. A hazardous waste incinerator proposed for an affluent suburb would, in all probability, meet with the same degree of unpopularity as a public housing project. Some of the objectors might well be the same, though this is far from guaranteed. But the *probability* of an incinerator developer making such a proposal is far smaller precisely because the opposition would be so predictably intense. The community, unlike a poverty-stricken inner-city area, would have ready access to both funds and professional volunteers who could tie up the proposal in regulatory proceedings for years. It would also be nearly impossible for the developer to argue persuasively that such a facility would enhance local economic development.

This simple fact has led advocates for the poor and minorities to note that waste management operators tend to take the "path of least resistance" in seeking sites for various kinds of waste treatment, storage, and disposal facilities. There is evidence to substantiate their claim. The United Church of Christ's Commission on Racial Justice, in a 1987 study, *Toxic Wastes and Race in the United States*, performed a statistical analysis of the locations of the nation's hazardous waste sites. After controlling for other variables such as urbanization and socioeconomic status, the study found that the single most important variable determining the location of such facilities was race—primarily the presence of an African-American or Hispanic community nearby. More recently, Native Americans have fended off a wide variety of proposals for solid and hazardous waste facilities on reservations. Vendors have been attracted largely by the fact that tribal sovereignty shields facilities from more stringent state regulation.

As charges of environmental racism have gained attention in public policy debates, skeptics have raised some cautionary notes about the nature of the evidence. Which came first, they ask, the toxic waste site or the people living nearby? In many cases, some note, the site did not originate as a dump per se, but as a welcome industrial facility that eventually fouled its own environment, but not without providing jobs along the way. While this is an issue that necessarily must involve case-by-case analysis of a site's history, it is equally clear, not only in the case of Native American lands but also in the prevalence of illegal dumping in inner-city neighborhoods, that the pattern of waste finding disadvantaged minority populations is real and must be addressed.

Opponents of the LANCER incinerator project in Los Angeles discovered a 1984 consulting report produced for the California Waste Management Board by Cerrell Associates, *Political Difficulties Facing Waste-to-Energy Conversion Plant Siting*. The report, by advocating that incinerator developers "take the path of least resistance" by targeting low-income, older, and poorly educated neighborhoods, confirmed everything LANCER's opponents believed was true but that they were afraid to find out. The first of three LANCER units to burn Los Angeles's solid waste was slated for South Central, the same inner-city black and Hispanic area in which the 1991 disturbances occurred following the state-court verdict that exonerated several Los Angeles police accused of beating Rodney King. (APA even had some indirect involvement in the LANCER debate, giving an AICP student award to the UCLA Graduate Program in Urban and Regional Planning for its research report for the Concerned Citizens of South Central. The report attacked the LANCER project and was considered instrumental in its downfall.) The Cerrell report subsequently gained wide circulation among opponents of trash incineration nationwide.

The Challenges

For planners and policy makers, the gauntlet has been thrown down. A variety of newly minted environmental and neighborhood groups backed by blue-collar and minority constituencies are nursing grievances. Their complaint is that they are bearing disproportionate burdens of environmental risk based on their racial or socioeconomic status. The challenge is twofold: first, to reduce the overall load of toxic and hazardous environmental burdens; second, to improve the siting process to make the distribution of truly necessary facilities more equitable, both in perception and in fact. Ultimately, this is a mission

that planners can fulfill only if they successfully cultivate a broad base of public support. Without public support for better policies on *both* these questions, the long-term result will be regulatory gridlock. In some jurisdictions, this impasse is already occurring.

An Ounce of Prevention/A Pound of Control

One thing is already clear on the first point. Local and state governments, as well as the federal government, must be prepared to exercise enough authority to carry out a meaningful pollution *prevention* strategy. The U.S. EPA already has an Office of Pollution Prevention, for example, but it is currently a purely voluntary program, unlike the mandatory pollution *control* regulations that have been in place for two decades. According to a 1986 Office of Technology Assessment report, *Serious Reduction of Hazardous Waste*, less than one percent of the $70 billion U.S. annual investment in pollution control was directed to waste reduction. The reason is simple. Mandatory pollution prevention steps over a line that industry traditionally has fiercely defended—the autonomy over the production process that it sees as part of its ownership prerogatives. Pollution controls, on the other hand, merely dictate limits on the effluents that emerge from the end of the pipe or smokestack.

However, this approach has tended to result in merely shifting pollution from one medium to another. The hazardous waste disposal crisis largely materialized when industry was barred from releasing the substances to the public's air and water. But the material must go somewhere. Landfills are, of course, unpopular. But banning land disposal of hazardous waste leads to incineration, which in turn produces one more technology targeted for protest by those who are asked to live near it. Moreover, incineration does not make things magically disappear. An ongoing issue concerning the industry has been the proper disposal of the toxic ash residue that results from the process. Meanwhile, disposal costs skyrocket, although many environmentalists would argue that they still do not reflect the true cost to society of wasteful industrial practices. Planners must take the lead in reexamining the entire concept behind this environmental merry-go-round.

It is no longer enough for planners merely to concern themselves with siting issues when putting a waste-handling facility somewhere is merely the rear end of a much larger societal problem. Demonstrating vision requires that our profession probe the roots of the problem. The

Mr. Emanuel's Tires . . .

Norman Emanuel, a Native American who owns the Emanuel Tire Co., is a highly respected innovator in the tire recycling field. In 1986, he began to store steel-belted tire shreds on an industrially zoned vacant lot in the Bridgeview neighborhood of west Baltimore. The neighbors, moderate-income African-Americans living in well-maintained rowhouses, initially welcomed Emanuel, but by 1987 began to object as the tire pile grew to 150,000 cubic feet while he sought expanded markets for his product and developed a new procedure to separate the steel and rubber. Neighbors feared the vandalism, blight, and health problems the tires created.

As the issue grew, so did the involvement of the city's planning, fire, and health departments. In 1990, Mayor Kurt Schmoke, recognizing the service to the community that tire recycling represented, appointed an interagency Mayor's Task Force on Shredded Tires to develop strategies to address the needs of all parties to the dispute. New state and city laws strengthened the regulation of tire storage, recycling, and cleanup. City and state officials negotiated a consent decree that allowed Emanuel to remove the tires without suffering a financial burden that might have led him to abandon the site. Emanuel and the neighborhood residents eventually achieved a mutual understanding that included his help with a neighborhood beautification project. (Source: Charles C. Graves, Baltimore's Director of City Planning; for information, contact Lois C. Matthew, President, Bridgeview Neighborhood Association, 2344 Riggs Ave., Baltimore, MD 21216.)

tools already exist to do this. Planners must use imagination in implementing them.

For instance, in controlling industrial hazardous waste, local governments can update their industrial performance codes to require toxics use reduction audits, not only as part of the site plan review of proposed facilities, but for existing businesses as well. Such audit services already exist, but municipalities can drive the demand for them in a way that purely voluntary efforts by industry never will. With the potential for accidents and leakages, there is no question that this is a matter of public health and safety. Already, the provisions of the 1986 Superfund Amendments and Reauthorization Act have created a structure under which local governments, solely or jointly, must form local emergency planning committees with the power to review mandatory reports on the storage of such materials at industrial and commercial facilities. Source reduction takes the process one logical step further.

This need not be a confrontational issue. Numerous states have already established waste-reduction offices in their environmental agencies, and many also support university-affiliated or nonprofit entities engaged in waste-reduction research. Many such programs have shown that local industries can become more profitable and competitive through waste-reduction efforts, although waste reduction efforts should not be made to depend on such results. But that prospect can help planners sell the institutionalization of such audits and the implementation of their recommendations as a win-win scenario for both industry and the environment. In the process, they will reduce the need for treatment, storage, and disposal facilities and the siting battles that regularly accompany them.

Saving Jobs

Waste-reduction activists have learned, however, that merely requiring waste reduction is not always enough. Sometimes the production process changes that are required entail substantial investments. For large companies, this may not be an insurmountable problem, but for the numerous small enterprises that dominate such industries as electroplating, it can be a matter of economic survival. For them, local, state, and federal governments need seriously to consider alternative financing mechanisms that will facilitate environmental improvements. Low-interest revolving loan funds have been used for other sorts of economic development, and certainly the survival of small businesses that provide well-paid blue-collar employment is an important economic development priority. Municipal planners need to combine the efforts of environmental and economic development agencies to seek creative ways to solve this financing dilemma.

Two very different reports have tackled aspects of this problem in Chicago and Los Angeles. In November 1989, Chicago's Center for Neighborhood Technology convened a conference of environmental and economic development activists to consider strategies for sustainable manufacturing. In its subsequent report, *Sustainable Manufacturing*, the center outlined the economic problems facing inner-city manufacturers, including small electroplating firms in Chicago, due to the costs of environmental compliance. It found that 79 percent of Chicago's industrial jobs were in shops of 50 or fewer employees. Similarly, a Cleveland study found that 94 percent of that area's industrial firms employed fewer than 100 people.

Meanwhile, students of the UCLA graduate program performed a study of air pollution problems for neighborhood clients. In *Improving Environmental Quality: Community Empowerment in East Los Angeles and Santa Fe Springs*, they found the air quality problem in East L.A. traceable to a poor pattern of land use in which auto body repair and auto painting firms were peppered throughout a highly populated Hispanic residential neighborhood. There were solutions, such as switching to high-volume, low-pressure paint spray guns, which increase the efficiency of transfer from applicator to surface and reduce the emissions of volatile organic chemicals.

Taking their cue from their clients, the students called for phasing out only the most incompatible land uses, while providing financial and technical assistance for numerous other small businesses that provide vital employment to a poverty-stricken neighborhood. In short, the residents of East L.A. know that the tradeoff between environmental quality and jobs is a false one. It can be obviated through appropriate remedies to help small businesses, the engine of the area's industrial economy, over the financial hump of achieving more efficient and environmentally sound modes of production. Inner-city neighborhoods need *both* economic development and a healthy environment. Wiping out the industrial base of the inner city by simply tightening the vise of traditional pollution controls will lead only to the sort of economic deprivation that makes waste facilities seem like the last desperate hope for salvation. As a matter of simple justice, no community should have to make that choice.

Creating Jobs

America has trouble making its garbage disappear. New York ships it to Ohio; Philadelphia ships it to Virginia; Central Islip's garbage barge becomes homeless on the high seas; and regulatory trouble strands a garbage train in downstate Illinois. No one wants to live near a sanitary landfill, and very few communities will tolerate the presence of a waste-to-energy incinerator. Is there any silver lining in this solid waste planning dilemma?

Some of the same planning principles that apply to hazardous industrial waste apply also to municipal solid waste—reduce, reuse, recycle. It is harder, of course, to alter consumer buying habits than to change production processes. And it is no mean feat for government at any level to convince merchandisers to alter their packaging habits, even though packaging has contributed mightily to America's burgeoning load of solid waste.

Nonetheless, serious progress has been made in some areas. Plastics manufacturers are beginning to take seriously their responsibility to find ways to recycle their products; a high percentage of aluminum cans is now being recycled; and some jurisdictions are instituting recycled-paper requirements for local newspapers, while enacting purchasing preferences for recycled materials for government use.

All of this has generated a substantial new recycling industry, some of it operated by municipal public works agencies, and some of it managed by for-profit and nonprofit recyclers. In places like Seattle and New Jersey, communities are beginning to recycle as much as half or more of their municipal solid waste stream. In the process, new job opportunities are being created. Planners now have a golden opportunity to combine environmentalism and community development. By targeting recycling facilities for economically disadvantaged neighborhoods, the unwanted jobs connected with landfills and incinerators can become the wanted labor-intensive jobs of sorting and processing recyclables. California, with multiple objectives in mind, has already developed a prototype of what such an effort could like. The California Integrated Waste Management Board designates recycling market development zones as a way of attracting companies interested in turning recycled materials into marketable products.

Planners should advocate bringing home to these neighborhoods the full value-added benefit of such operations. A 1992 report from California's Local Government Commission, *Capturing the Local Economic Benefit of Recycling: A Strategy Manual for Local Governments*, provides a road map of techniques for accomplishing this. As it notes, "a ton of loose office paper can be sold for $30. Bale the paper and the market price rises to $150. Pulp the paper and the market price reaches $570. Convert the pulp to writing paper and the price can climb to $920 a ton."

In other words, it is not enough simply to produce a few jobs by locating a transfer station in a needy area. Communities must decide to use the value-added aspects of recycling as a strategic opportunity for economic development while these programs are still in their infancy. This poses also the possibility of using our economic development resources to train minority entrepreneurs for these emerging businesses. Converting our garbage from an eyesore and health threat into new manufacturing jobs for depressed areas should go a long way toward ameliorating the sense of environmental injustice such communities now share. Furthermore, that challenge to policy makers is immediate. In another decade, many of these initial phases of the development of our recycling infrastructure will be behind us.

Again: In Whose Backyard?

Once the nation has seriously committed itself to the business of reducing the environmental threats posed by its excessive generation of hazardous and solid wastes, it must still resolve the question of environmental equity for those facilities that are absolutely necessary under any circumstances. We live in a modern industrial society that generates medical waste, nuclear waste, chemical waste, and solid waste, and some portion of that will always be inescapable and require appropriate disposal. Of course, regulatory agencies must apply the strictest standards possible to ensure maximum protection of public health and safety. But governments at all levels must also seek ways to ensure some equity in the sites that are chosen for this purpose.

Equity, of course, makes a great battle cry for activists but a very slippery concept for planners and other decision makers to implement. Any point system or rating system will be heavily laden with unavoidable value judgments. What is important, however, is the public perception that there is at least a genuine attempt to balance the burdens of environmental risk that communities are asked to share, much as they are now asked to share the responsibility for affordable housing in New Jersey and Connecticut. It is the perception that no one cares that drives much of the current environmental anger in low-income and minority communities.

Equity Action Agenda

There are four areas for potential action that would help to resolve this problem.

First, Congress must come to terms with the impact of a series of U.S. Supreme Court decisions that have ruled that waste of any kind is an item in interstate commerce whose interstate movement, therefore, cannot be restricted by state law. Amid the intense economic pressure to find inexpensive disposal sites for waste, the practical impact of these decisions—most recently in *Chemical Waste Management v. Hunt* and *Fort Gratiot Landfill v. Michigan Department of Natural Resources*—is to make nearly impossible any meaningful state-level planning concerning adequate capacity for local wastes. If landfill and incinerator operators can import waste from anywhere in the nation, how can local planners assure their communities or regions that the next facility built will be the only one necessary to take care of the area's problems for a given period of time? Ironically, given the Court's conservative leanings, the only answer is for the public to own all such facilities and choose its own customers on an entrepreneurial, rather than on a regulatory, basis. One state, Delaware, has already adopted precisely this approach.

What can Congress do? The U.S. Supreme Court has left open the opportunity for Congress itself to authorize state limits on the importation of interstate waste. After all, the interstate commerce clause, on which these cases are based, reserves to Congress the power to regulate interstate commerce. Some in Congress have pursued precisely this question. The issue was a vital part of the debate in 1992 over reauthorization of the Resource Conservation and Recovery Act. APA supported the inclusion of state solid waste planning provisions in that reauthorization, but Congress in the end failed to act on the bill.

Of course, safeguards against abuses of state authority should be built into the legislation. Delegation of authority to states to restrict importation should be made contingent upon adequate planning by the state to handle its own waste, probably subject to plan approval by the U.S. EPA. There is already a variation on this idea in the federal legislation authorizing interstate compacts for the storage and disposal of nuclear waste, an arguably more knotty problem in terms of public perceptions and fears. No state should be able to ban importation while failing to take care of the waste generated in its own backyard. But this statutory framework would allow for a reasonable degree of certainty in state plans and capacity projections and alleviate the justifiable impression that some states, particularly in the Midwest and South, are serving as the nation's dumping grounds.

Second, the nation must also come to grips with the perception that some areas are absorbing a disproportionate burden of environmental risk, regardless of equity among states on the waste issue. Waste facilities are not the only environmental threats that communities fear, and environmental burdens are seldom distributed equally within states. On a nationwide basis, APA should seriously review the concept behind the Environmental Justice Act, originally introduced by Sen. Albert Gore, Jr. (D-Tenn.), who subsequently became vice-president. Rep. Cardiss Collins (D-Ill.) has taken the lead in promoting this legislation in the House, and in February 1994, President Clinton issued an executive order that imposes on federal agencies, including the EPA, the responsibility to take environmental justice into account in their siting decisions. The Gore bill attempted to establish some criteria for deflecting new hazardous facilities from the 100 most highly impacted areas in the nation, as determined under a point system to be used by the U.S. EPA, with the list to be approved and published by the EPA administrator. These measures recognize the historic tendency of environmentally noxious enterprises to cluster in low-income, economically depressed areas that then forfeit the opportunity to attract other, more environmentally benign industries. In other words, "bad industry drives out good."

Third, this same concept can be applied at state and local levels through siting laws and "fair share" ordinances. New York City has pioneered in this area with its relatively new fair-share criteria adopted in the 1989 city charter revisions. While it may still be too soon to render a final judgment on the success or failure of New York's experiment, there can be little doubt that the spirit of the New York law represents an honest effort to tackle a long-standing perception of inequity in the siting of both public works and human services and low-income housing facilities. Previously, without such criteria, the political perception was that it was every borough (and neighborhood) for itself. While such politics may never completely disappear, at least there is a sense that if one borough accepts an undesirable land use today, it will be someone else's turn tomorrow. Of course, while much of the New York law is geared to the peculiarities of governing the nation's largest city, the conceptual framework is nonetheless adaptable to other cities and counties across the country.

Finally, in all of this, there can be no substitute for genuine citizen participation, the subject of another paper (by William Klein) in this urban agenda package. The public track record for soliciting and incorporating citizen concerns has often been at its worst on environmental issues. The technical nature of many of the facilities, the heavy dependence of government agencies and the courts on scientific expertise, and the sheer complexity of some issues have combined to exclude the input of citizens, particularly those from organizations representing low-income communities, until projects reach a more clearly political stage. Then, policy makers and developers vent frustration when politicians respond to angry constituents by stalling or canceling long-planned projects like dams, power plants, and incinerators. It should be obvious to everyone that something is not only amiss, but very inefficient, in this entire process.

There is a better way. Starting from the broadest possible definition of an environmental problem, officials should *at the outset* endeavor to involve *all* affected constituencies in developing credible solutions. It will no longer be enough to ask only for input on the rear end of a problem—for example, where to site an incinerator and how large it should be. The real problem may be how to reduce the volume of waste generated, how best to preserve the value of recyclables during collection and processing, and what financial benefits can be gained by pursuing, in the broadest sense, the most socially cost-effective solutions. Not only might policy makers find community activists helpful in developing creative solutions, but the public education benefit of such interaction would undoubtedly prove far higher than that of any alternative. In the end, there is likely to be no greater aid to sound environmental policy making and implementation than the involvement of a public that is knowledgeable and confident of the value of its own input. For the most part, the alternatives have led to stalemate and stagnation. We can do better.

Jim Schwab is a senior research associate with APA and the editor of Zoning News *and* Environment & Development. *He is also the author of* Deeper Shades of Green: The Rise of Blue-Collar and Minority Environmentalism in America *(Sierra Club Books, 1994).*

4

Economic Development: Partnership, Innovation, and Investment

By Nikolas C. Theodore and Marya Morris

Headlines from newspapers in our nation's largest cities tell the story of America's difficult economic times: U.S. auto plants relocate to Mexico; thousands of unemployed workers line up for hours in bitter cold for several hundred jobs at a hotel; the world's largest retailer lays off thousands of employees.

The roots of economic crisis are complex and far reaching. Deindustrialization, and the awkward shift from a manufacturing-based to an increasingly service-oriented economy, has shaken the very foundation of America's economic strength as mobile capital, competing in global markets, has replaced heavy industry as the dominant form of economic power. In many regions, the shift to a service-based economy has driven down average wages and made a second family income almost an imperative for owning a home and maintaining a decent standard of living.

The current recession has made it clear that the service sector—the source of most of the job growth during the 1980s—will not be the economic savior it has been touted to be. This sector has been affected more severely in the current economic downturn than in any previous recession. Although economists are debating the causes of service-sector decline, much of the problem can be traced to the overbuilt real estate market, decreased consumer spending, and lowered demand for new homes. For the first time, the core industries of the service sector—finance, insurance, real estate, and law—have made deep payroll cuts at both the partner and associate level, not just at the support staff level.

Patterns of economic growth and decline have been uneven, and certain segments of society have been especially hard hit as economic opportunities vanish with the closing of area businesses. Urban centers, in particular, have undergone dramatic changes in employment, occupational structure, and industrial location. In many areas, the decentralization of the metropolitan labor force, combined with the uneven spatial distribution of business growth and decline, has had devastating effects on inner-city neighborhoods. These changes find large numbers of minorities and the poor residing in urban areas plagued by disinvestment and the deterioration of local employment and business opportunities.

Short-sighted economic development policies at every government level have made the process of economic restructuring more painful than it might have been. Federal, state, and local governments have yet to design coherent policies that increase homegrown capacity as a way of addressing the persistent unemployment, mounting business failures, and widespread disinvestment that have accompanied deindustrialization. Instead, economic development policy has centered on luring mobile capital from other areas by using generous incentive packages. This emphasis on competition between localities and redistribution of economic activity, rather than increasing homegrown capacity, has made economic development a zero-sum game with few winners and many losers.

Traditional Economic Development Policy

Traditional public-sector approaches to encouraging economic development have emphasized stimulating employment growth and the diversification of the local tax base by promoting the establishment or relocation of branch plants, attraction of corporate headquarters, and the redevelopment of downtown business districts. Initially, public-sector responses to economic decline centered on devising and marketing location incentives to attract outside firms.

Location incentives can be grouped into two categories: 1) general incentives for development, which are inducements broadly available throughout a state or locality, and 2) geographically targeted incentives to stimulate investment in selected areas.

The Forms of General Incentives for Development

Tax policy. Governments have two tax policy tools at their disposal, the general tax structure and tax incentives. The general tax structure determines the rates and burdens imposed on individuals and businesses throughout a jurisdiction. States and to a lesser extent, localities have latitude in determining tax structures and to what degree upper-income individuals or private-sector firms, for example, will shoulder tax burdens.

Tax incentives are used by governments to alleviate some of the impacts of the general tax structure on selected businesses or classes of individuals. Tax incentives most commonly take the form of exemptions or credits to encourage or reward certain types of investment by the private sector. For example, numerous cities offer deferred tax payments and tax abatements to firms to encourage relocation.

Debt financing. Historically, state and local economic development programs designed to attract mobile capital or retain in-state businesses have concentrated assistance on the provision of debt financing. Debt-financing programs are loan programs that subsidize a portion of the costs of capital through low- or no-interest loans, loans with favorable repayment schedules, and revenue bond financing. These inducements are marketed to private industry in an effort to influence location decisions.

Regulatory policy. State government has considerable regulatory power over a range of functions which directly influence the cost of doing business in a particular locale. States' regulatory powers influence, among other things, environmental regulations, wage rates, and banking practices. Compliance with state regulations, particularly those concerning the environment, may prove costly to business. However, regulatory policy has widely been manipulated by state governments as an inducement to private industry.

Labor incentives. Labor incentives offered by state governments differ somewhat from the other general incentives for development. While tax policy, debt financing, and regulatory policy directly influence the costs of locating in a particular state or locality, labor incentives indirectly reduce the costs of doing business. Labor incentives primarily influence work force availability through right-to-work laws that reduce union influence, job training legislation that prepares the work force for new occupations, and unemployment and disability insurance laws that place varying costs on industry.

Geographically Targeted Incentives

In addition to general incentives for development, the public sector uses various geographically targeted incentives to attract businesses to particular locales:

Enterprise zones. Enterprise zones are created to reverse urban decline by removing disincentives to the private redevelopment of economically depressed or underdeveloped areas. Depending on the particular program, businesses locating in designated enterprise zones are eligible to receive tax benefits, favorable zoning changes, moratoriums on minimum wage laws, and amendments to building codes.

Site development incentives. Site development programs are used to acquire and prepare parcels of industrial and commercial property for prospective businesses. Through these programs, a portion of the costs of land development are subsidized by the public sector. Site development programs can be distinguished from general programs that subsidize business location costs.

General development assistance programs make subsidies available to firms interested in relocating anywhere within a state or locality, whereas targeted site development programs allow public agencies to predetermine business location during the land acquisition process.

Infrastructure improvement assistance. Infrastructure improvement assistance programs are used to attract or retain industrial and commercial investment in distressed areas. Areas that have experienced severe business loss are redeveloped to suit the needs of industrial or commercial concerns with the hope of attracting new business investment. Assistance, such as street and sewer improvements, is intended to improve the marketability of designated locations.

The Failure of Traditional Policy

Traditional economic development policy has been called into question in recent years. One reason is the absence of definitive research to demonstrate that general inducements actually attract outside businesses or significantly increase the level of economic activity in an area. In fact, research on plant location determinants clearly shows that the most important considerations for firms making relocation decisions are size of local population, migration patterns, transportation rates, local purchasing power, labor productivity, wages, and union control — location characteristics and factors that are largely beyond the control of state and local governments.

The most important reason, however, for the demise of traditional economic development policy making is that many states and localities continued to experience accelerated economic decline despite the proliferation of policy tools designed to attract and retain mobile capital. The Midwest and Northeast, once home to the largest and most productive heavy industry in the world, became characterized as the Rust Belt following plant closings and widespread capital disinvestment.

Many areas in the South and West experienced rapid economic growth as the result of the relocation of businesses and industry from other regions, only to experience decline as the pace of capital flight abroad quickened. States and localities that had once attracted mobile capital through location incentives lost these same firms to Latin America and Asia. These movements made it clear that capital mobility presents threats to economic expansion that cannot easily be tempered by traditional economic development policy.

Second-Generation Economic Development Policy: Building Local Capacity

As the effectiveness and popularity of traditional policies diminished, planners began to experiment with programs to stimulate economic development in noncompetitive ways by encouraging the creation and expansion of local businesses. Strengthening local resources as the source of economic growth began to be seen as an alternative to attracting mobile capital and promoting interstate relocations. In this way, economic development policy has undergone a shift from an almost exclusive reliance on location incentives to stimulate investment, to an

Partnerships: The Federal Empowerment Zones and Enterprise Communities Program Is Not Business as Usual

The Clinton administration's Empowerment Zone/Enterprise Communities (EZ/EC) program requires all applying communities to prepare a community-based strategic plan for revitalizing their most distressed neighborhoods. The program will provide in excess of $100 million to six urban and $40 million three rural Empowerment Zones and $2.96 million to 65 urban and 30 rural Enterprise Communities.

Either type of designation will allow the community to issue tax-exempt bonds to finance purchases of land and business properties, given them special consideration when competing for funds under other federal programs, and will allow the community to waive certain federal requirements.

Although the basic premise of the EZ/EC program is similar to enterprise zones (targeted financial assistance coupled with tax incentives) , the emphasis on forging new partnerships sets it above and apart from previous federal neighborhood revitalization programs.

- Through the strategic plan, the community must outline a framework for revitalization that stipulates how federal funds will be used and how social services and economic development initiatives will be brought together to address the most pressing problems in their community.

- Applications will be judged in part on the extent to which the individuals and organizations that will potentially benefit or be affected by a designation are involved in the strategic planning process. Whereas previous efforts only gave lip service to the notion of grassroots involvement, HUD will be looking for clear evidence of participation.

- The plan must provide proof of secure financial assurances from the private sector. This could be a bank agreeing to participate in a revolving loan fund for entrepreneurs to a large employer agreeing to provide job training for area residents. The application then will be judged on the degree to which the community can use the public investment to leverage additional private investment.

approach that seeks to stimulate economic expansion in under-used industry sectors and geographical locations.

The capacity-building approach to economic development policy was born out of the realization that there is not enough mobile capital available to satisfy the economic growth needs of every state and locality. To stem decline and renew expansion, planners are turning toward local economies as a source of economic growth. Where traditional economic development policy was characterized by interstate competition as jurisdictions vied with one another to attract distant firms, second-generation policy emphasizes the creation and development of homegrown enterprises.

Redefining the Public Sector's Role in Economic Development

The evolution of state and local economic development policy has resulted in a redefinition of planners' roles in stimulating economic growth. In an effort to ameliorate the effects of deindustrialization and decline, state and local governments have become risk-takers actively involved in identifying investment opportunities. As a result, policy making has become a more complex undertaking that requires planners to engage in entrepreneurial activities, including partnership, innovation, and investment.

Partnership. Second-generation economic development policies are designed to improve the capacity of businesses to meet internal and external demand for products and services. Priority is placed on identifying needs that new or existing local enterprises can satisfy. In the role of partner with the private sector, planners conduct various activities, including the identification of market opportunities, advertising and promotion, and analysis of local demand. While these activities were previously considered to be exclusively the responsibility of the private sector, this shift in policy is the result of private investment being denied to industry sectors and locales that are deemed to present poor investment opportunities. Planners have undertaken these activities to stimulate private investment in potentially profitable enterprises which offer benefits in the form of increased employment, tax revenue, and local spending.

Innovation. Innovation, the development of new ideas, is the cornerstone of economic growth. It is through innovation that firms develop competitive advantages in their markets. While innovation occurs primarily as a result of private-sector activities, the public sector increasingly encourages technological change and specialization by providing financial and technical assistance to entrepreneurs.

Investment. Second-generation economic development policy emphasizes using relatively small amounts of public funds to leverage larger amounts of financial capital from conventional lending sources. Whereas traditional policies targeted large-scale enterprises with established credit histories for assistance, second-generation approaches seek to increase private investment in sectors that historically have been denied capital. Because of the aversion of the private sector to risk, the focus of policy has shifted to expanding credit availability to potentially profitable ventures that yield an expected rate of return. This approach presents a departure from traditional policy, which provided direct assistance using public resources. Under traditional approaches, state and local economic development budgets were exhausted after making only a handful of loans. With the rise of second-generation policy has come the creation of innovative financing instruments that allow public funds to be "recycled" and, consequently, serve far more businesses.

RECOMMENDATIONS

Partnership

Strategic planning. Planners are increasingly using a strategic planning framework to set economic development policy and build bridges to the private sector. Strategic approaches seek to increase private investment in sectors that historically have been denied capital. Because of the aversion of the private sector to risk, the focus of policy has shifted to expanding credit availability to potentially profitable ventures that yield an expected rate of return. This approach presents a departure from traditional policy, which provided direct assistance using public resources. Under traditional approaches, state and local economic development budgets were exhausted after making only a handful of loans. With the rise of second-generation policy has come the creation of innovative financing instruments that allow public funds to be "recycled" and, consequently, serve far more businesses. Planning has been used to achieve numerous goals, including identifying the most effective uses of public resources; providing a mechanism for public-private cooperation; educating the public; and developing multi-year priorities that target growing industries.

"Buy Local" programs. Planners are beginning to experiment with "Buy Local" programs designed to keep dollars within a jurisdiction by promoting the purchase of locally produced goods. In developing these programs, planners assemble directories of local businesses, develop linkages between producers and consumers, and assist firms in meeting local demand.

Job training. The nation's educational system has not produced a workforce that can compete in new global markets while maintaining an increased standard of living. A widening "capability gap" requires that planners make use of Labor Market Information (LMI) to better tailor the skills being taught with the skills being sought by employers. State development agencies and nonprofit economic development research groups can provide planners with LMI on occupational trends, job growth in specific industries, and location of employment opportunities.

The economic problems facing inner-city residents are compounded by an educational system that has failed to prepare many to compete in a changing workforce. In addition to providing technical skills training, job training programs must be prepared to offer clients basic skills development in arithmetic, reading, and writing.

Innovation

Technology modernization. States and local governments should undertake activities that stimulate entrepreneurial development and modernize firms in their jurisdictions. Shared manufacturing centers, national manufacturing technology centers, university-based science parks, and high-tech councils have all been used with varying degrees of success in achieving economic development goals of job creation, industrial retention, modernization of manufacturing facilities, and diversification of the economic base.

Small business incubators. State and local governments have recently added small business incubators to their lists of economic development tools to assist homegrown enterprises. Public-sector incubators are an important tool for promoting light manufacturing industries, oftentimes allowing for their location in vacant industrial facilities. In this way, business incubators are used by planners to develop new firms in areas where older industry was once located. Small business incubators offer firms four advantages: 1) on-site assistance in obtaining financing and

---

Innovation: Technology Commercialization Programs

More than 200 local government programs promoting scientific research, technology transfer, and innovative development are in existence. These initiatives include shared and national manufacturing centers, technology extension services, federal laboratory technology transfer, science parks, and high technology councils.

Shared manufacturing centers, for example, contain state-of-the-art, flexible manufacturing equipment systems that can be leased to firms that can not afford the equipment. The Massachusetts Microelectronic Center in Westborough is supported by a consortium of microelectronics business in the Route 128 corridor and area universities. It was launched with a $20 million state investment in the mid-1980s with two primary goals: giving university students hands-on training in the industry and an economic development tool that would support small and medium-size microelectronic firms in the Boston area.

Source: Diane Palmentiera, *Local and Regional Based Initiatives to Increase Productivity, Technology and Innovation.* Available from Innovation Associates, Inc. 1130 Connecticut Avenue, N.W. Suite 700 Washington, D.C. 20036.

---

preparing bids; 2) a real estate component that provides flexible space and below-market rents; 3) management consulting; and 4) support services. These advantages provide entrepreneurs assistance during the early stages of business development.

Job growth in sustainable communities. Protecting the environment and building a strong economy have long been viewed as mutually exclusive endeavors. This stems from the perception that environmental regulations are a hindrance to the United States's ability to compete in the global economy because they drive up the cost of doing business.

But many planners, environmentalists, and economic development professionals are now aware of the concept of sustainable development —that is, balancing the resource needs of the present generation without jeopardizing the ability of future generations to live and prosper. It has also become clear that a healthy environment can improve the quality of life in a community or region, and healthy communities are attractive places to do business. Planners can help balance environmental and economic development policies by promoting community-based job programs in areas such as recycling, air pollution abatement, wastewater treatment, and hazardous waste disposal.

Investment

Financial assistance to minority entrepreneurs. Increasing minority business ownership has been the goal of numerous federal, state, and local economic development policies. However, the results of these policies have often been disappointing. Minority business ownership rates continue to lag behind rates for whites, and minority-owned firms continue to be concentrated in industry sectors with the lowest average levels of profitability.

The fundamental problem facing the minority business sector is undercapitalization, which results in most firms remaining small, overleveraged, and concentrated in labor-intensive industries that serve neighborhood markets. To expand minority business opportunities, economic development policies must improve access to financial capital, particularly in the form of equity capital, working capital, and loan guarantees. Initiatives such as linked deposit programs can be used to increase the supply of capital available to firms. Public funds can be deposited in lending institutions with the condition that an increased number of loans be made to targeted groups.

Leveraging private investment. Increasingly, the public sector is using innovative financing instruments that allow funds to be "recycled" and serve far more businesses than has been possible under direct loan programs. Loan guarantees and revolving loan funds are examples of such programs. Loan guarantees from the public sector encourage lending by conventional sources by increasing the security of a loan and thereby reducing lending risk.

When a government backs a loan with a guarantee, access to capital is improved and, barring default, no claim on public resources is made. Revolving loan funds are loan pools that typically are capitalized through a one-time legislative allocation. When loans to businesses are repaid, the principal and interest return to the fund to be lent to other firms.

Infrastructure support for economic development. New infrastructure and local service improvements can sharply enhance the competitive position of existing businesses by improving delivery accessibility, expanding labor markets, broadening markets, and reducing business costs. This can create new opportunities for business expansion and location as well as generate thousands of construction jobs. Public investment in local telecommunications infrastructure can create new opportunities for back office operations for insurance, banking, records processing, and telemarketing.

Investment in transportation infrastructure can also reduce costs of delivery of materials and finished products, and improve access to employment centers. The federal government reasserted its interest in upgrading transportation infrastructure with the passage of the Intermodal Surface Transportation Efficiency Act of 1991.

Investment: Improving Infrastructure Helps Businesses

The Wisconsin Department of Transportation is expanding and building 200 miles of Highway 29, which will connect the cities of Green Bay, Appleton, and Wausau to Minneapolis-St. Paul. The project is motivated by economic development goals base in part on a survey of state businesses that revealed demand for improved east-west truck transportation routes to deliver food, lumber, and stone, glass and clay products.

Gas and electric utility companies have long been involved in helping local governments recruit industries to an area—now they are helping businesses to expand, as well. The Edison Industrial Hardware Rebate Program in Southern California and Central Main Power Co.'s Commercial Design Assistance Program are both assisting businesses in upgrading equipment technology through financial and other assistance for conversion to new, energy-efficient equipment that can enhance productivity, cost structure, and competitiveness.

Investments in telecommunications infrastructure are expanding location opportunities for back-office operations for banking, insurance, and telemarketing. With the move to fiber optic transmission lines (replacing copper cables), companies can move large amount of data very rapidly and are no longer tied to the headquarters location. These improvements have resulted in a boon for some suburban communities, as well as medium-sized cities and far flung exurban and rural areas, as many semi-skilled clerical jobs have been shifted out of high-rent locales.

Preferential funding treatment in the six-year, $151 billion appropriation will go to projects to upgrade existing road networks and to the development of alternative modes of transportation, such as public transit and pedestrian and bicycle facilities.

Finally, increased investment in large, regional hub airports and small general aviation airports can create business opportunities for airport-related service suppliers, shippers, and corporate users. Airport investment also enhances delivery of services and human resources.

Nikolas Theodore is the project manager for the Strengthening Business Opportunities Project at the Chicago Urban League. Marya Morris is a senior research associate at APA.

Planning for Human Services

By Frank So, AICP

Poor neighborhoods often have an extensive list of physical deficiencies: abandoned and burned-out residential structures; vacant lots that once contained structures, but now are debris-filled; boarded-up vacant commercial buildings along desolate strips; street lights that don't work; broken curbs and pothole-filled streets; sunken sidewalks; and so on. These neighborhoods are also often the site of profound economic and social problems: crime, drugs, alcohol dependency, homelessness, child-abuse, high teenage pregnancy rates, high unemployment, and inadequate medical care and day-care services.

Government's response to these problems has generally been characterized by a division between the physical environment on the one hand and the socioeconomic environment on the other through separate tracks in terms of programs and services. The physical problems are generally the responsibility of city governments and are planned and administered through planning departments, community development departments, and public works agencies. The social and economic issues are typically addressed by a wide variety of agencies in a complex network of government at federal, state, county, and city levels, in addition to a separate network of nonprofit and charitable organizations that deliver human services. In many, if not most, communities, these two service systems operate side by side without much knowledge of the other's activities, let alone coordination and joint planning between them. Given the enormous and growing need for improvement in the quality of the lives of inner-city residents, coupled with the generally declining fiscal resources available to both sectors during the 1980s and early 1990s, this situation demands new comprehensive approaches. In many cases, the two sectors are serving the same groups, individuals, and neighborhoods.

Bridging the Gap—Partial Efforts

A more comprehensive, coordinated approach to bridging the gap between physical planning and human services is clearly in its infancy. Perhaps it is an oversimplification (we cannot readily prove it because of a lack of literature), but it appears that the human services field is characterized by a great deal of fragmentation into specialized interests.

The Columbus-Ohio Metropolitan Human Services Commission (MHSC)

One early effort to build a communitywide, human services planning and resource-allocation system among social service agencies was the Columbus-Ohio Metropolitan Human Services Commission (MHSC) that was developed to create a planning system to allocate resources from the then federal block grant and revenue sharing programs (Connell 1983). The objectives of the MHSC were: to analyze funding and policy decisions; identify services to be maintained, reduced, or terminated; formulate alternative funding sources; determine appropriate service delivery strategies; and develop an advocacy role at the state level. (Source: "Dealing with Fund Reductions through Interagency Contingency Planning," by David A. Connell, in Robert Agranoff, *Human Services on a Limited Budget*, Washington, DC: International City Managers Association, 1983.

For example, there is a strong tendency for human service organizations and agencies to be single-purpose ones. The boards and staffs of these agencies tend to focus almost exclusively on their agendas. Parts of the field, particularly social workers working with inner-city families, have become increasingly aware of how a single poor family may be faced with numerous problems including unemployment, lack of training, juvenile delinquency, drug addiction, and health problems. Such social workers struggle to help families solve multiple problems.

Most of the planning in the human service field takes place within individual agencies. Planning is characterized by a heavy emphasis on needs assessment of a particular client group and figuring out how to make funds stretch to meet those needs. During the 1980s, these agencies had to deal with declining federal and state grants, and engaged in a lot of cutback planning and budgeting. New sources of funds, such as user fees, private contributions, and public-private partnerships were increasingly sought and used.

During the late 1980s, urban planners, city managers, and city finance officers, in a few places, began to experience a growing awareness that their traditional scope of activities relating to physical facilities and services left out something extraordinarily important—the human services dimension.

A number of city managers began to struggle with such concepts as redefining "infrastructure" to include programs that affect people. One community, for example, realized that a housing program had to focus on the needs of the children who lived in the housing. Many communities have established programs related to homelessness. Savannah, Georgia, established a neighborhood services program focussed on the "desperate lives of underclass families." The program focussed on affordable housing, an urban youth corps program, a youth futures program, and a variety of other efforts to go beyond the traditional concern with clean streets and repairing water lines. As these city managers began increasingly to deal with municipal expenditures on social services, a concept of "human infrastructure" was conceived. Given the managers's focus on traditional operating and capital budgeting systems, it is not a great leap to think about investing in human services—especially in an era of scarce fiscal resources (ICMA 1990).

In 1990, Temple University Press published *Making Equity Planning Work: Leadership in the Public Sector* by Norman Krumholz and John Forester, which described Krumholz's tenure as planning director in Cleveland between 1969 and 1979. His experiences were extensively discussed at national and state conferences and in the *Journal of the American Planning Association* during that decade. As the title suggests, the entire planning program was oriented toward assessing the costs and benefits of an entire range of Cleveland planning actions and capital improvements on the poor. What is notable is that the authors and the publisher felt this to be a worthwhile venture in the early 1990s. That is, even though the book describes events, issues, and processes that took place between one and two decades ago, the book does not read as though it were history. Not only are the problems of many central cities similar to Cleveland's, but, in many cases, they have become worse. Obviously, the authors and publisher believe there is little evidence that planning agencies throughout the nation have been particularly more responsive in reorienting their programs in social and human terms, as Cleveland did in the 1970s.

While a lot of leadership in the Minneapolis system came from the finance department, the problems facing the City of Minneapolis caused Oliver E. Byrum, its widely respected planning director, to write *Old Problems in New Times: Urban Strategies for the 1990s* (APA Planners Press, forthcoming), which is a provocative statement that, in effect, demands a new and expanding focus for central city planning. The book provides a planner's perspective on the relationship among physical, economic, and social issues. Special attention is paid to such issues as metropolitanwide approaches to alleviating poverty, how market and public policy affect inner-city conditions, how to improve the livability of low-income neighborhoods, and the jobs-housing-transportation linkage issue.

As large cities update or revise their general plans, it is likely they will increasingly focus on human services in addition to the traditional land-use, public facilities, and transportation systems. For example, the 1989 Denver Comprehensive Plan had as one of its "core goals" that

> [T]he City must help the disadvantaged help themselves. In an
> increasingly complex society, the disadvantaged population
> includes the poor in population segments such as the disabled,
> inadequately educated, the elderly, the homeless, the develop-
> mentally disabled, teenaged mothers, single parents and those
> with substance-abuse problems.

The plan goes on to recommend a variety of reforms and steps relating to the welfare system, breaking the poverty cycle, and better support of services to the disadvantaged. For example, a new policy council will provide planning community linkages to the Department of Social Services. Another proposal was to study the feasibility of a metropolitan health care system for lower-income residents.

Unified Services Planning and Budgeting in Minneapolis

In the late 1980s, Minneapolis, typical of many central cities, began to face a number of problems simultaneously, including growing drug and crime problems in its neighborhoods, deteriorating infrastructure placing a strain on the city's resources, declining funding availability, and growing socioeconomic dislocations that required new and expanded local services. Thus, in 1989, the city began to design a new unified service planning and budgeting concept. It was aimed at establishing a long-term interagency service planning process, which would ultimately integrate service planning and budgeting. The city had a sense of confidence based on its experiences in the preceding years with growing cooperation among a variety of agencies serving the same constituencies. Interestingly, the Minneapolis Capital Long-Range Improvement Committee that had been in existence for 20 years, served as the planning system. Key city agencies included the departments relating to planning, policy, and finance, as well as independent agencies representing parks, libraries, schools, and county boards. The strategic service planning process requires all departments to focus on a directions framework document and a neighborhood revitalization program. All agencies coordinate their efforts through a common policy board. The process structure also includes an implementation committee and neighborhood involvement through neighborhood workshops. A program director assists the policy board. (Source: John Gunyou, "Unified Service Planning and Budgeting: The Next Generation of Service Management," *Public Budgeting and Finance*, Fall 1991.)

Metropolitan Human Services Investment Strategy

In 1990, the Atlanta Regional Commission—the metropolitan planning agency—completed its "Human Services Investment Strategy," a culmination of a several-year effort by an agency responsible for physical planning to expand its concern to an entire array of social and human service programs in the region. A 14-member coalition, representing a wide array of city and county governments, the Chamber of Commerce, the public schools, private development agencies, the state, the United Way, and others, used a strategic planning process to measure the need for social services, the degree to which various agencies were providing them, the declining sources of funds, and the prioritization of investments. The program studied a wide array of public human services expenditures on education and employment, health, housing, and the family. The program dealt with day care for low-income families, hospitals and public health centers, literacy, affordable housing options, mental health, the mentally retarded, services for alcohol and drug abusers, personal care homes, psychiatric hospitals, emergency shelters, and other human service programs. In addition to preparing information and evaluation systems, looking at various incentive programs, and creating community awareness, the program developed a list of specific expenditures by the governments and agencies involved in the program. This list was arranged in tabular form, much like a capital improvements program and budget. Goals were identified, strategies were suggested, time frames were specified, estimated funding and sources of funding were specified, and lead agencies were identified (Alliance for Human Services Planning 1990).

An effort similar in its mission to the Atlanta Regional Council's program was instituted in the Twin Cities area by the Metropolitan Council (Anderson 1991). The council's leadership felt that, while its mandate had always been stated as "physical, social, and economic needs," much had been done, in fact, in the area of physical planning but only some on social and economic needs.

To redress that balance, the council has begun developing what it calls a "human investment framework." The goal is to prepare a blueprint or guideline that will help the region in allocating financial resources in the future dealing with human needs. The project asks three basic questions:

- Are we, the region, effectively and efficiently investing in our people?

- What should we change in our human investments?

- What regional policies should guide these investments?

The Twin Cities project will begin by getting all of the governmental, nonprofit, and citizen organizations involved in developing a program. The program will develop information about human service investments in the region by population and location; the amount of financial resources committed to various sectors; demographic change; social issues (e.g., crime, drug use); the effectiveness of investments in achieving goals; and the amount and nature of future investments that can be made, given the shrinking pool of resources.

There are several significant characteristics of these two efforts:

1.   Two agencies with strong histories in physical development planning have expanded the scope of their interest to include human services because these issues increasingly cannot be separated from the future well-being of their respective urban communities.

2.   While the agencies themselves do not have operational responsibilities in providing human services, they do have considerable experience using an organizational framework that is adept at bringing various interests together—interests that represent different sectors of the community (i.e., public, nonprofit, private, and citizen).

3.   The effort is an areawide, metropolitan effort that defines the problem as everyone's responsibility—not just the central city, but all of the metropolitan area.

4.   The analysis and focus have a financial perspective; that is, they do not amass long lists of things to do and then figure out whether they are affordable. Rather, they make some upfront assumptions about likely levels of funding available and then allocate resources based on priorities and need.

5.   Funds that are spent are defined not as "expenditures," but rather as "human investments," and *people*, especially those in trouble, are defined as *resources* that are as important as any physical resource. The efforts clearly declare that investment in them will have a future pay off that will benefit them and the community.

6.   Finally, the efforts use the tools and concepts of the planning field, including strategic planning, involving all interest groups, determining missions, setting goals, developing criteria for priority setting, and, most importantly, borrowing the concepts of capital improvements programming and budgeting. What was used in the past to determine expenditures for streets, sewers, fire stations, and parks, is not also being used to analyze and give priority to investments in the entire range of human services.

Implications for Planning

A relatively thorough literature search in the fields of planning, city management, local government finance, and human services, along with contact with major national associations, resulted in the documentation of the few human services investment planning efforts cited here. Nevertheless, our much greater knowledge of the massive problems confronting the poor and disadvantaged in many of our urban communities convinces us that the planning field simply must move more vigorously in expanding the scope of the work of planners and planning agencies in local government and at the metropolitan level into human investment strategic planning. The need is overwhelming. The delivery system is extremely fragmented. The resources being allocated are shrinking. *Planners responsible for comprehensive planning can no longer ignore the most important needs and issues that affect the quality of life in inner-city neighborhoods and ultimately the social health of the community as a whole.* It does no good to invest in physical facilities if the underlying social infrastructure is deteriorating. In some instances, the investments might better be shifted from physical to social investments with greater benefit to all.

The debates within the field in the late 1960s and early 1970s about social planning and urban planning were inconclusive but leaning toward a socially sensitive physical planning. For example, environmental impact statements sometimes deal with the impact on low-income groups; or, California planning enabling statutes provide that local communities may have social elements as an optional element. Many individual planners have carried out their strong interest in social issues by going to work for human service agencies, being particularly interested in inner-city neighborhood planning issues, or perhaps being interested in low-income housing or housing the homeless.

Based on the evidence, it can be fairly said that the planning field still is overwhelmingly interested in its traditional physical subject matter. True, the number of economic development agencies in local government has grown over the years, and these are aimed at creating jobs. Yet, they have usually paid little attention to the needs of people who do not currently have jobs.

Nevertheless, the handful of examples cited show that at least some planning agencies feel compelled to expand their programmatic interests to include the human service dimension, particularly in its allocation of financial resources among the wide variety of service programs competing for funds.

In the past, when the scope of the planning field was debated, some argued about either the competence of planners to practice in new specialties for which they had no training, or they agreed that the traditional physical work program was important enough to receive all our attention. As regards the first argument, we needn't worry excessively because planners will not take over the detailed planning or operational responsibilities. Instead, they will use their planning skills involving citizen participation and financial planning tools to help the other specialists and elected officials do a better job in meeting human service needs. In terms of the latter argument, we can no longer take the position that investments in the physical community alone will improve poor people's lives. The poor people of this country who have historically been poorly served by their government institutions and their elected officials don't define the elements that contribute to a higher quality of community life so narrowly. Neither can planners.

Frank So is the American Planning Association's Deputy Executive Director.

Social Impact Assessment Sensitizes Planning

By Sandra Lee Pinel, AICP

*Public planning, ostensibly concerned with problems overlooked in the
private sector, ironically has no systematic technique for assessing the
social equity of its own actions. Social impact assessment seeks to
provide such a mechanism.*
William Rohe, 1982

INTRODUCTION

Two fundamental aspects of our profession, no matter what topic we
work on in which rural or urban setting, are serving the public interest
and being concerned with the total quality of life. Yet we cannot
effectively address either of these purposes if we do not understand the
diverse groups affected by our plans and the dynamics of social
change.

Many planners deal with land use and economic development. They
are accustomed to thinking of social planning as the responsibility of
health and social service agencies or the United Way. But understanding the social context and impacts of plans is not the same as planning

for social services nor is it the same as including a social element in a comprehensive land use plan. It is the social impact of all our work in transportation, land use, economic development, and capital improvements that must be considered.

There are notorious examples of such impact in our collective professional history. Urban renewal projects of the 1960s razed or divided entire neighborhoods for the construction of highways and office complexes. Exclusionary zoning affected the cost of housing. Currently, there are cases of how the revitalization of historic downtown areas gentrifies what were functioning ethnic neighborhoods and markets, and of how large lot zoning, intended to preserve rural character, resulted in scattered urbanization rather than continued farming. Controversies over urban redevelopment, logging moratoriums, water supplies, and rancher's rights in the West have put the spotlight on the real consequences of planning and regulations on households.

We may not deliberately analyze and deal with the social impacts of our work, but we are acting as applied social scientists every day. Our actions alter the fabric of communities. We cannot plan for the public interest if we do not understand the values, perceptions, and likely actions of the various "publics." Increasingly, we try to work for a diverse set of public interests.

We have two basic choices. Either we can make assumptions about those social values, systems, and behaviors in response to the plans we consider or recommend, or we can try to find out what those values, social systems, and behaviors are. I argue in this paper that using the second approach will not only make us more sensitive to the impacts of policy, but also result in more effective plans and projects, appropriate to the context and likely to be implemented.

This paper will cover two topics:

- The uses of social impact assessment

- The social perspective in all phases of the planning process, especially in designing an effective citizen participation process

There are perspectives and methods from anthropology and other social sciences and there are tools from the practice of social impact assessment that we can use throughout the planning process from goal setting to evaluation. These principles and approaches are illustrated with some examples from New Mexico, and the reader is referred to additional examples.

WHY SOCIAL IMPACT ASSESSMENT?

Because local communities, even small ones, are diverse places, planners must serve many constituencies. Understanding social diversity and responding to social change are keys to effective physical planning.
Howe, 1988

Both the City and County of Santa Fe are changing rapidly. Elected officials and citizens raise the question: How can we have equitable development that is good for natives and less harmful development? This is the dilemma. The City of Santa Fe was established before the pilgrims landed and is located in a region of ancient and sustained pueblo Indian cultures. The ambience and culture of the region attract newcomers and raise costs. The new mayor of Santa Fe, elected in March 1994, has promised that tourism and development will be evaluated for benefits across segments of the community, and some types of tourism will not be promoted. The previous mayor was known for promoting tourism without restraint.

Tensions in gentrifying Santa Fe neighborhoods are high. Windows are shot out in some neighborhoods. Tensions increased over the past five years as housing prices have risen to a median of $180,000 (up 20 percent in the first three months of 1994 alone). Added jobs have paid minimum wage in the restaurant and service industries. The gap between the average family income of $22,000 and the cost of living continues to grow. The county area bordering the city is filling with mobile home parks, the only housing many who work in Santa Fe can afford.

Realtors describe the historic Santa Fe Plaza as the hottest commercial real estate in the country. But local residents, some half of whom are from Hispanic families who count their history in centuries, have abandoned the plaza. Of the basic food, clothing, and hardware stores of 10 years ago, only Woolworth survives. The lease rates are too high for many retailers.

The development of Santa Fe's railroad yard is looked to as a possible alternative central gathering place. It is located only a half mile from the Plaza. The city spent money for a developer to design a site plan, which proposed high-density offices, commercial areas, and residences. Adjacent neighborhoods objected and insisted on a new plan to serve community needs.

Development pressures go beyond the city limits of Santa Fe. Since 1970, 75 percent of the growth in the area has been in the county. The historic farming village of La Cienega, 12 miles south, raised vehement objections to a golf course resort development after a modified plan was approved by the county. The affected acequia (irrigation ditch) association was satisfied with a revised development and mitigation plan to minimize environmental impacts, but other La Cienega residents later objected, saying that the impacts were on the very cultural identity of the community. At one hearing the county commission was checking for guns at the door and wondering why these protestors waited until after the project was negotiated. The community has organized its own planning effort and is calling on the county to develop a specific social impact assessment step in its review of development proposals.

There is a basic economic and environmental impact aspect to what is happening in Santa Fe. But the social and cultural impacts are even more important in predicting how people will react to proposals. Both the city and the county have spent a great deal of money on feasibility studies, site plans, and negotiations with developers for projects that residents perceived as detrimental to the basic character of the area. Money would have been saved if local governments initially invested in some social and cultural observation and surveys to get a handle on the perceived "tradition" or "quality of life" that villages and neighborhood groups are so vehemently trying to protect. The problem is not as simple as growth vs. no-growth. Growth is seen as benefitting newcomers only. No-growth might have the same result. County and city officials are searching for appropriate development and for a way to maintain traditional village, agricultural, and other ways of life.

The case of Cochiti Dam, located on the lands of Cochiti Indian Pueblo, also points out the importance of anticipating how a local community will react to or participate in a development. Cochiti Dam and the Town of Cochiti Lake were constructed along the Rio Grande in the 1970s. To ensure that the 1,000 residents of the pueblo would have jobs or income from construction of the dam, the Bureau of Indian Affairs developed a sketch plan for a recreational community and helped negotiate a 99-year lease of 6,000 acres of tribal land near the lake. The pueblo was to receive lease fees in addition to having an agreement with the U.S. Army Corps of Engineers to run the lakeside campground.

The environmental impact statement projected many social benefits, such as jobs and Indian-owned business. However, the master plan rested on faulty social assumptions concerning Cochiti Pueblo's values and available human resources for the anticipated entrepreneurship that would result in jobs. Eventually, the developers of the recreational community and the pueblo went to court over alleged misrepresentations, and the 250 town residents were caught in the middle (Pinel, 1988).

What were the faulty social assumptions? First, projected jobs were dependent on Cochiti Pueblo people having the skills and institutional capacity to manage business enterprises. Second, the plan ignored the cultural value of the resources that were destroyed, which turned the Pueblo against the project. Cultural resources included ancestor villages, a sacred rock important to a number of tribes, and farmland destroyed by a rising groundwater table below the dam. During years of meetings, the tribal council affirmed the cultural importance of these resources and rejected managing the campground or allowing a secondary hydroelectric development. The pueblo has a development corporation that took over the master lease and revenues have increased. But conflicts over how to use the recreational facilities—for tribal members, town residents, or for-profit rentals—continue.

Many American Indian tribes have taken the position that developments cannot be considered beneficial unless their own cultural perspectives on quality of life and environment are the basis of that evaluation. For example, one Arizona tribe located adjacent to rapidly growing and water-hungry Phoenix directed all federal agencies managing its land to "develop methods and procedures which will ensure that the integrity of this community and its Indian culture and values may be given appropriate consideration in decision-making along with economic and technical considerations" (Stea and Buge, 1982).[1]

Recently, ranching and resource dependent counties are also claiming the right to evaluate social impacts—social impacts of environmental regulations. The county lands movement by western ranching and timber dependent communities challenges federal land-use plans and species protection laws. Catron County, New Mexico, has a land-use plan that includes a statement of "custom and culture," a social impact statement relating to federal logging and grazing policies, and a land-use ordinance asserting primacy over federal and state actions. The county is demanding to be partners in land-use decisions affecting their way of life, refusing to be restricted from that land by "environmentalists." Planners cannot afford to ignore such movements as reactionary. Rather, we can try to understand the values and issues at stake and help parties find middle ground.

The issue of affordable housing may be the most widely known illustration of the need to consider the social impact of planning and zoning. The increase in single-parent households and elderly households and the rising cost of housing in "well planned" communities forces us to question the premise of single family zones so that accessory apartments and other uses are allowed (Pollak and Gorman, 1989; Ritzdorf, 1987).

The need for social sensitivity may be understood in cases of minority communities, but the danger of making unquestioned assumptions about social values or change also exists in the bread-and-butter practice of land-use planning, zoning, and housing development. We are challenged to learn about changing community dynamics and to help elected officials make decisions based on vision and social reality, not just on a cookbook of ordinances. We have the ethical responsibility to point out diverse values and differential impacts.

WHAT IS SOCIAL IMPACT ASSESSMENT?

As with environmental or economic impact assessment, social impact assessment (SIA) is the evaluation of policy alternatives in terms of their estimated consequences (Finsterbusch, 1980).

> *Social impacts are* "the consequences to human populations of public or private actions—that alter the ways in which people live, work, play, relate to one another, organize to meet their needs and generally cope as members of society. The term also includes cultural impacts involving changes to the norms, values and beliefs that guide and rationalize their cognition of

themselves and their society." (Interorganizational Committee
on Guidelines and Principles for Social Impact Assessment,
1994)

Some SIA studies focus on policy alternatives, and others on "events" or
projects. Planners employed in public agencies often deal with both
long-range plans and policies and the review of particular projects. In
both types of situations, SIA can be a tool to focus public debate on
social consequences, alternatives, and trade-offs (Carley and Bustelo,
1984).

How a "social impact" is defined and the methods for documenting one
differ widely. Four themes are prominent:

- Identify different groups within a planning jurisdiction or project area and learn their concerns and quality-of-life values as a
  basis for evaluating positive and negative impacts.

- Base predictions on an understanding of the dynamics of community change and the interrelationships between groups and
  larger systems.

- Develop factors to note impacts on social cohesion

- Integrate social and technical research with the political process
  and participation of the affected groups in choosing among
  trade-offs.

Social impact assessment work in the United States first evolved from
the National Environmental Policy Act (NEPA), in which large physical
projects had to be evaluated for their impact on population growth,
community facilities, transportation, and neighborhood character as
those factors were related to environmental impacts. Other laws such as
the American Indian Religious Freedom Act and the National Historic
Preservation Act require some social or cultural assessments. Most SIA
has been done at the point when a specific project is proposed for a
specific location. Its use in policy development is recent and the literature scarce. However, the 1994 guidelines published by a team of
experts from various agencies do address policy development (Interorganizational Committee, 1994).

Some planning documents equate SIA with economic and fiscal impact analyses, presuming a public benefit of increased employment or public revenues but ignoring the unequal distribution of such benefits among income groups or neighborhoods.[2] A positive project is assumed to be one that generates more public revenues than public service costs. Social benefits are not a goal subject to analysis in these studies but simply a secondary factor (So, 1988).

Wal-Mart, for example, may increase jobs and the tax base but destroy the small businesses that glue the downtown together. Job and income multipliers will not show the secondary loss of downtown viability or the social function of the local coffee shop. A common mistake in evaluating economic impacts of new establishments is to assume that all jobs will accrue to the planning area, whereas they may be regional or gained at the expense of local small businesses (Hustedde, Shaffer, and Pulver, 1988).[3]

NEPA requires assessment of social impacts such as employment, demands on social services and facilities, and changes to the population and tax base. However, often only one public interest is assumed and winners and losers are not specified (Finsterbusch, 1980). The question of perceived impacts and changes to social cohesion and inter-relationships within minority or other sub-communities are seldom mentioned. Yet those are the vary impacts that matter to the mayor of Santa Fe, who wants development that will create more equity and sense of community in the city. Indicators of equity and other goals are needed in a form that can be used consistently in development review processes.

Early SIA was limited to anticipating or measuring against indicators for public facilities; housing; income; crime rates; morbidity and infant mortality; social, health, and educational facilities; and perhaps attitudes. More recently, there is a focus on variables to assess the *dynamics* of social change. A project or policy can result not only in an economic loss or gain, but in social severance—the rupture or impairment of relationships between people and places (Stanley and Rattray, 1978).[4]

SIA is a tool with which we can assess plans first from the perspectives of those directly affected by the action, then from the perspective of the government interest (Armour, Bowran, Miller, Miloff, 1977). Community concerns are documented, whether or not an outside expert considers those issues significant. The role of the person doing the SIA is to bring out assumptions and test technical plans against the perceptions of affected groups.

SIA is also a tool for addressing the different needs of impacted groups, the bureaucracy, and politicians (Carley and Busetlo, 1984). If groups do not come forward in the political process, we can use social methods to learn of their concerns and avoid faulty assumptions we might otherwise make about resident responses.

SIA Steps Parallel the Planning Process

1. Determine how the study will be used in the policy or plan review process.

2. Define the goals against which the policy or project will be evaluated—local, federal, state, neighborhood. State assumptions that are being made about human behavior.

3. Examine social dynamics, systems, trends in which the policy or project will operate, and define factors and indicators.

4. Identify affected groups and use scenario building or other techniques to analyze primary and secondary impacts for each factor and cross effects on other aspects of community life.

5. Involve public officials and affected groups in deciding which are acceptable and unacceptable risks and how important each is.

6. Consider other alternatives, trade-offs, and mitigation actions.*

The range of options is greater if the SIA is done early while policies are projects are being designed, rather than after investments have been made in one alternative.

For instructions and tables to guide an SIA process see: Finsterbusch 1977, 1980; Wolf, 1977; Armour, Bowran, Miller and Miloff, 1977; Canan and Hennessey, 1982.

---

* For a full flow chart and description of each step, see The Interorganizational Committee, 1994.

There is a tendency to think of social or cultural impact assessment as something necessary only when dealing with Indian tribes or ethnic groups, but the perspective is important in a range of everyday situations planners deal with. It may not be necessary or feasible in every case of planning to do a full social impact assessment, but there are four reasons to use a social impact perspective and to scan potentials and problem areas from that perspective:

1.   To define the "publics" to ensure equity
2.   To improve the quality and appropriateness of plans
3.   To improve the chances that plans will be implemented, not derailed
4.   To mitigate effects

In any project approval process or general plan, we can pause to question our own assumptions:

- *What are the purposes and anticipated results of this effort?*
  As planners concerned with equity, we can ask whose purpose a plan is intended to serve and whether we are erroneously assuming that all groups will be served.

- *What are the boundaries of the impacted area?*
  It is helpful to know if the residents perceive boundaries in the same way planners do and if functional communities correspond with or are divided by those boundaries.

- *What consultation process should be used to reach those self-identified groups?*
  Understanding how a culture or group is likely to respond to different participatory settings is critical. Lack of response to a notice of public hearing or lack of Hispanic women's vocal participation in a meeting should not necessarily be interpreted as lack of interest or input. Different input processes will work with different groups.

- *What types of information will be used to identify problems and evaluate alternatives?*
  Data divided into subject areas is biased against a holistic community system perspective. Rather than being trained to look at all factors of family and community life within a limited geo-

graphic area, planners must often use aggregated jurisdiction-wide data on households, transportation, and economics. It can be difficult to draw the connections in terms of social change.

• *What local knowledge, customary behaviors and traditional institutions can be used to design implementation or mitigation strategies that are feasible?*
In addition to economic and political feasibility, there is "social feasibility" of a plan or project. Will human beings act the way we assume they will in response to the plan or ordinance? As discussed earlier, Cochiti Pueblo residents were not prepared to participate effectively as entrepreneurs in the development of Cochiti Lake and so neither the pueblo nor the town realized the anticipated economic benefits.

• *What are the local criteria against which groups of citizens will evaluate success or failure of the plan or project?*
Values are fundamental to evaluating positive and negative outcomes. In addition, a planner can best evaluate why certain aspects of a plan or policy worked or did not work if he or she understands how to observe human behavior and decision making and to understand diverse values. If we are concerned with equity, we need to elicit the criteria from those communities against which success will be measured. A social perspective will also indicate reasons for plan failure and directions for improvement (Pinel, 1991).

Within each phase of the planning process, there is a need for social information—values for problem analysis and so on. SIA is a systematic guide to making sure we pause to obtain and consider that information (Pinel, 1979 and 1991).

WHEN TO USE SIA

Planning practice in the City and County of Santa Fe requires SIA. Santa Fe residents are asking for social impact assessments, but what do they exactly mean? The City of Santa Fe discouraged a permit request for the construction of a mega food store in a district with similar developments on the grounds that the store does not hire union workers and does not create the type of jobs or economic development that Santa Fe desperately needs for its residents. The current zoning

and subdivision ordinances have no provision for making such judgments.

In Santa Fe County, communities are asking the county to develop a
social impact assessment tool that would be used as part of the development project approval process. One of the goals stated in county
meetings is to maintain traditional villages and acequias (irrigation
ditches). La Cienega Village residents are pushing for a system that
would prevent the type of resort development recently approved, not
only on the grounds that it would use water rights, but that it would
change the character of the community.

If the county were to incorporate performance criteria into its zoning
ordinance or development review process, it could pre-screen proposals
and make recommendations to developers before final plans are submitted. There are cities that have adopted a checklist either as an
informal staff aid or as a part of performance review standards. However, the indicators of input were not defined. These checklists have to
be based on a clear set of public policies such as "affordable housing"
against which proposals can be judged and a list of criteria for "quality
of life" (Lauber, 1977).

A preliminary social impact assessment checklist can save the local
government and the developer money, whether or not it is required by
state law or local ordinance. Before investing substantial funds or time
in a project, they can make sure nothing major is overlooked or discov-
er whether a more detailed SIA might be necessary.[5] The City of Santa
Fe had to recommission an expensive design for the railroad yard
because the first one did not meet the basic neighborhood and resident
image of what was needed in that part of town.

At the state policy level, the New Mexico Rural Development Response
Council is considering the development of an SIA checklist to red-flag
state policy changes, such as school consolidation, which might impact
on the sustainability of rural communities in the state. To create such a
checklist, however, the indicators of "cost" and "benefit" need to be clear
and they will differ depending on the community one is working with.
A vague question such as, "Will the project improve the quality of life?"
is useless without clear statements of what that means to the community. The SIA process used with one project can help local governments
"plug into" local data and frames of reference so that communities or
groups can better define their values and goals and react effectively

with outside agencies by spelling out the effect of proposed actions on those goals (Meredith, 1992). The question of how these village or ethnic goals become part of public policy is a separate social equity question.

SAMPLE CHECKLIST			
NEIGHBORHOOD GOALS	Rail Yard Sketch Plan #1	Rail Yard Sketch Plan #2	Rail Yard Sketch Plan #3
Diversify Economy			
Develop affordable housing and home ownership			
Improve wages and job security			
Maintain older residential neighbor-hoods and encourage home businesses			
Promote mixed use			
Create gathering spaces for locals			
Increase business investment in human resources			

A checklist can be used to highlight and discuss the impact of policies or specific project proposals. Public goals such as "affordable housing" or "maintain downtown businesses" are the basis for the categories (which can be weighted) and focus groups or interviews with groups or neighborhoods are the basis of indicators. The checklist on sketch plans brings out criteria and allows for improved design. Specific criteria and indicators can be used in performance review ordinances. If precise impacts need to be noted, research has to go into the indicators and the evaluation of direct/secondary, short-term/long-term, and local/regional impacts.

If the project needs more scrutiny, one SIA technique is to list each group's goals, including the public goals, on one axis of a matrix and the impacts on the other axis. Then note whether the proposed action or policy would advance or erode the goals of each interest group. In addition to anticipating changes, one must plan for how they will be evaluated and ranked as positive or negative. Rather than doing a traditional cost/benefit analysis that quantifies all impacts, a qualitative approach lists all impacts so that they can be ranked by the public according to different community viewpoints. Once the differences in perspective are visible, it is possible to deal with trade-offs (Hill, 1968).[6]

A planner might recommend community meetings to address concerns. In other circumstances, if the local government has made a political or financial investment, the only option may be mitigation of effects. The SIA will give the planner necessary information to anticipate the feasibility of such mitigation measures. The point here is not to make planners hire social scientists or spend more time on social impact assessments. The point is to be transparent and deliberate about assumptions, sources of data, and the "community" whose interest one serves and to provide a setting for discussion and negotiation (Vlachos, 1982). If new alternatives are not possible, the SIA clearly documents what affects should be mitigated, and these actions can be budgeted into the implementation plan. It is best to assess a possible set of alternatives early on, before a lot of technical work and expense has been invested (Cramer, Dietz and Johnston, 1980; Rohe, 1982).

When to Hire a Social Scientist

When understanding social realities may mean the success or total political failure of a plan or policy, a social scientist working with the planning team can be a good investment. It is best to consult with that person early on, when the planning process and participants are being decided and the goals being elicited or to make the social scientist part of an interdisciplinary team that is engaged in supplying information to the planning agency. This might be baseline information, a survey of community needs and goals, an evaluation of alternatives, or mitigation actions.[7]

Local officials are usually unfamiliar with SIA and the usefulness of a social scientist in contrast with someone who has "hard" skills such as engineering. However, some initial social research may be the best investment a planning agency can make if it saves money on detailed

Applied Anthropology

The planning profession is dedicated to helping communities cope with and direct change. Social and cultural anthropologists study the nature of community and the dynamics of change so that an SIA is based on understanding a complex systems of interrelated community and regional activities. Social anthropology is uniquely suited to the planning perspective because it focuses on holistic community studies, understanding how different groups make decisions within their environments and the role of values and risk perception in decision making (Rohe, 1982, p. 372-373.) Applied anthropologists can also offer methods to make plans more appropriate:

1. Use cognitive mapping to identify communities' and groups' geographic boundaries and special places.

2. Design focus groups and interviews to identify local meaning of statements such as "preserve neighborhood character."

3. Design meetings or surveys so that particular cultural groups will respond.

4. Build more realistic scenarios of alternatives based on social network analysis and household decision analysis.

5. Elicit values for predicting perceived benefits and costs of different actions.

6. Undertake basic community studies as reference for identifying social networks and local knowledge that can make programs more feasible.

7. Evaluate what went wrong to revise plans or ordinances.

For information on applied anthropology research methods, begin with Pelto and Pelto, 1970, and Partridge, 1984.

project studies that are irrelevant or harmful to segments of the public. One early effort was by the City of Cleveland, which incorporated social equity concerns into basic policy statements for city development. When a social impact assessment revealed adverse effects on parts of the population, the staff worked to redesign alternatives to create more benefits for those in need.

How values are assigned is key to choosing between alternatives and it is key to ensuring that planning is sensitive to the needs of different groups. Improving the quality of life is one of the most fundamental goals of planning and yet the hardest thing to define. Daniel Lauber's review (1976) of local government assessment checklists indicates that planners were not using any system of identifying indicators. However, SIA was relatively new at the time. Methods have since been developed for interviewing residents to identify indicators that are more meaningful than the commonly used ones of jobs or tax base.

Planners can start by going back through records of community meetings, highlighting value statements, and—with the help of a social scientist—using focus groups to develop criteria to be used in evaluating alternative plans.[8] Anthropologists can help because their methods focus on the community as the unit of analysis, the dynamics of social change, and the relationship of one aspect of life to another.

The problem with the Catron County Plan mentioned earlier is that the "custom and culture" statement about the value of grazing and forest products to the community is not based on good methodology, and so it will be difficult for it to be accepted as legitimate in challenges to U.S. Forest Service land management decisions. If one wants to stop an action based on "custom and culture," that custom needs to be documented for each separate group within the community. Catron County is now using NEPA guidelines to become part of the federal planning process.

SOCIAL PERSPECTIVE IN THE PLANNING PROCESS

The tools of SIA are not limited to assessing a project. We can incorporate social and cultural factors into all steps of the planning process. Project review information can help in policy and plan development.[9] The standard textbook process includes a number of steps (not always sequential) that involve balancing technical work with political process:

1. Establish planning scope, process, and participants.

2. Elicit vision, problem statements, and goals.

3. Analyze the demographic, economic, and land/water use trends and issues.

4.   Prepare overall policies that guide development.

5.   Develop and evaluate alternatives to achieve policies such as development guidelines, zoning ordinances, community development corporations, and so on.

6.   Implement, evaluate, and revise plans.

Planning is effective if it leads to innovative and realistic solutions that fit the local context, are implemented over time, and benefit "the public." The Pueblo Indian tribes of New Mexico provide some good examples of how elected officials, administrators, and planners can develop better plans by taking local values, perceptions, behavior and knowledge into account.

During a decade of working with Indian pueblos and other Native American groups, I participated in the search for culturally appropriate economic development enterprises. After using its comprehensive plan during 10 years of tribal development, the pueblo updated it in 1990. The original planning committee members were included in updating process.[10] Zia Pueblo is used in the following section to illustrate how to effectively place cultural concerns at the center of a development strategy.

Establish Scope, Planning Process, and Participants

The Zia Pueblo tribal administrator was careful to include the tribal council, which is composed of the head of all households, and keep councilors informed of how any action relates to the plan and policies they approved. The tribal council does not change. All households have representation, whereas, tribal officials change semi-annually.[11] Given the focus on community equity at Zia, the tribal administrator made sure that projects were not perceived as his idea and that the community as a whole used the plan.

Before proceeding with a designated planning commission, we should scan the community to identify the groups that could be impacted or whose behavior could influence whether or not the plan will be successful. At Zia, the "community" was easy to identify. In contrast, in the previously mentioned case of a resort development in the Village of La Cienega in Santa Fe County, inclusion of the local acequia association was insufficient. Other residents insisted on involvement when negotiations with the developer were being finalized.

Viewing the township or other locally defined "community" as a social system, we can better identify stakeholders. If a regional plan is for an area where people do not identify with "the region," consider creating it as a synthesis of each county or village plan. Many planners must develop jurisdiction-wide plans and find the public does not attend the meetings. A social or scan of the community first asks: who are the groups, why are they not participating, and how can that group be approached through other methods.

Goals, Problems, and Policy Statements

The recent practice of "visioning" has made planning more grounded in local values. This is a great improvement over older plan documents that began with data analysis and problem statements without stating the values of the community. There is no "problem" unless someone attaches a value to the event or trend. Processes that bring forth people's own statements of vision and issues make values and value differences visible.

Mail surveys and public hearings are inadequate to solicit values because the agenda or the survey form predetermines what will be discussed. From the very beginning of the goal setting process, we need to find out what the frames of reference are for the different groups within the community. It is my experience that once those "communities" have been identified, involving them separately or collectively in a visioning process is effective. Zia Pueblo used a visioning workshop to rewrite the goals in its comprehensive plan.

In a participatory planning process developed by the Institute of Cultural Affairs West, (an international nonprofit group specializing in facilitation methods for organizational development), the vision workshop starts with a question, "What will this community look like in 10 years if it develops as you feel it can and should?"

As part of brainstorming, each table of participants writes ideas on cards that are placed on the wall. Participants are asked to group ideas according to similarity or association. The facilitator does not start with the assumption that there will be separate goals for "land use," "social services," "economic development," and so on. The participants talk about how youth delinquency is related to farming, for example, until each group of ideas is given a name that captures a part of the vision.

When the Zia Pueblo planning committee used this process, the section of the plan initially named *Agricultural Resources* became *Continue Zia Life Ways*. The section on *Natural Resources* became *Conserve Wildlife and Land for Future Generations*. The vision gave community meaning to the standard and lifeless goal statements such as "encourage carefully researched economic development projects." With clear value statements from the vision, the pueblo has a basis against which to evaluate alternative economic development ideas for the benefit or cost to the quality of life.

A second method is to "articulate the contradictions that block the vision." In analyzing its own barriers to economic development, Zia Pueblo did not want business development on tribal land, but only off-reservation. It was felt that there was a fundamental conflict between the full-time demands of running a successful business and the cultural demands on tribal officials for community and religious activities. A business would be more successful as an off-reservation investment that brought income into the pueblo to be invested in more appropriate community development strategies. With clear priorities, the tribal council undertook a number of successful projects including purchasing commercial land in a border community for business development and becoming involved in the New Mexico film industry.

Uncovering inherent contradictions such as between "preserve tradition" and "economic development" forces new alternatives. Planners can use the process of evaluating a proposal to bring out the same value conflicts. We can ask decision makers why they do or do not want an idea implemented. A focus group around this question could be planned separately with each impacted group and then planners could mediate the development of a new alternative.

The way background data is compiled also affects how relevant the plan is to social issues. For example, a regional planner may be able to choose between evaluating data on employment, transportation, and so on in aggregate for the region, by county, by township, or by ethnic group. It is when employment is related to transportation, for example, that we can pay attention to social impacts. Data on demographics, critical environmental areas, land-use trends, and other areas can be brought before different neighborhoods or groups to clarify issues and priorities. More detailed studies of conditions are then guided by the categories of perceived importance (Cramer, Dietz, and Johnston, 1980).

Develop and Evaluate Alternatives

If they are to be implemented, ordinances, development projects, and the like should be internally feasible from a social and cultural standpoint, as well as from the standpoint of market, law, or public cost. Some social research can result not only in more equitable plans, but in plans that will work within a specific context. In the case of Cochiti Lake, the anticipated benefits were based on wrong assumptions about what would be required for tribal participation. Existence of a regional market for recreation and retirement did not make those benefits automatic.

An ordinance can be designed to take advantage of traditional attitudes. Zia Pueblo asked the Bureau of Indian Affairs (BIA) to study the range and recommend solutions to an overgrazing problem. BIA range technicians were invited to present their findings to the entire tribal council meeting. The BIA recommended a standard permit fee based on the common theory that increased cost leads to decreased use. However, a traditional Zia land management principle is that all families should have equal access to tribal resources for subsistence use. Some tribal council members thought the fee would result in more access for the wealthier families, whereas, most families need a few cattle to reduce food costs. Instead of a fee, the tribal council suggested a total limit on permits to be equally distributed among tribal members. They also questioned some of the technical data on carrying capacity. Elders offered to do site visits with technicians to monitor results.

An ordinance impacts on social and economic relationships as much as it does on ecological practices. For this reason, it must be designed for the situation, not adopted from a text or neighboring community. Transfer of development rights, performance zoning, and PUD zoning tend to be adopted when in fashion. In Zia's case, the ordinance fit the culture. Any legal ordinance overlays a complex set of informal or unwritten laws that guide people's behavior. It is best to find out what people value and to use what people know about the place or land to find out what will be effective.

Participatory workshops are only one way. There are a number of other methods that can be adapted from anthropology and other social sciences in any phase of a planning effort.[12]

Plan Results and Revisions

How do we decide a planning effort was a success or failure? The decision depends on who gains and who loses. If we are careful to elicit values of different groups on the front end, we then have some criteria for monitoring impacts. We can also ask residents to evaluate what they have seen before or in a neighboring community. The rapid expansion of the tourist industry and second home market in Santa Fe has given neighboring communities an example to point to: "We don't want to be like Santa Fe!" The next question is, "What exactly don't you want, and why?"

Zia Pueblo looked at the tribes doing bingo on the reservation, decided Indian people were being affected, and said no. An SIA of an existing project or part of town provides the list of issues to consider in future development decisions.

The questions raised in social impact assessment help promote communication among planners, elected officials, developers, and groups of affected citizens on the real issues that will derail an ordinance or project later. SIA as part of the planning process, rather than as an afterthought, helps groups articulate goals and react effectively to planners and officials. In Santa Fe, for example, projects are being defeated not only because of "on the ground" impacts but because of a general perception that most developments are to benefit outsiders.[13] Public involvement strategies need to be designed to involve those who perceive they have an interest.

A social perspective that asks about actual community characteristics, relationships and dynamics is helpful in every phase of the standard planning process from identifying the problems to understanding what went right, what went wrong, and what to do next.

CONCLUSIONS

We are challenged to make planning an integral part of community development and a tool so that diverse groups can be part of determining the future of the community.

Making planning participatory is only a start. Who should participate and how do we reach those persons? Lack of direct participation in public meetings does not negate planners' responsibility to respond to diverse groups. Including a social element in a comprehensive plan also misses the opportunity inherent in our diversity. Human values are measures of effectiveness for land use, tax policy, housing, economic development, and other planning components. All have social consequences on a community's informal support systems, opportunities for youth, volunteer groups. The real question is how do we evaluate our impact on the quality of community life? What is quality of life to those in the community?

The specific steps in social impact assessment can be used to evaluate policies or projects so that assumptions about human needs and community dynamics are brought to light and debated and so that alternatives can be developed to address community needs.

The methods that help us elicit local values and define quality of life within an SIA are also useful in every phase of the planning process. By making values, local knowledge, social dynamics, and perceptions of the different publics visible, we can create plans that are more appropriate, feasible, and likely to be implemented. Anthropology has particular qualitative and community study methods that can help us sensitize planning practice.

The most important first step often left out of planning practice is questioning our own assumptions. Rather than using a cookbook approach, we can use methods for SIA and anthropology to design an appropriate process or project.

Planning practice is, by its very nature, a social intervention. We have the professional responsibility to understand the effects we may have by intervening and to give the best advice we can to decision makers. As a profession, we pride ourselves on our ability to take a comprehensive perspective and to synthesize the work of various experts to see the interconnections and big picture. We need partnerships with professionals such as anthropologists.

Few of us are social planners, but all of us must deal with the elusive and socially defined "quality of life." We must bring assumptions under the sunlight of scrutiny, and ask ourselves whose social goals we are working for, what are the social dynamics we are dealing with and what might be the actual results of a plan or policy on different groups within the community or region.

Our effectiveness is largely dependent on how well we understand social dynamics. SIA gives us a window through which to look at the more elusive and essential thing called "community."

What Can APA Do?

To promote socially sensitive planning using SIA, the American Planning Association can:

1. Facilitate a professional exchange between professional planners and social impact assessors at conferences and training sessions. In addition to the Society of Applied Anthropology, there is an International Association of Impact Assessment that meets annually.

2. Devote a PAS report or *Journal of the American Planning Association* issue to the topic and invite social impact assessors and applied anthropologists to write articles on how their work could improve the planning process.

3. Encourage cross training during graduate school in subjects such as urban anthropology and rural sociology.

4. Create an award category for innovative plans that address or build on unique social situations or which advance methods of socially sensitive planning.

NOTES

1. See Stoffle (1990) for a consultation process to evaluate impacts with Native American communities. Also see Geisler, Green, Usner and West (1982) for Indian SIA examples.

2. Fiscal impact studies have been defined as "a projection of the direct, current public costs and revenues resulting from population or employment change to that local jurisdiction" (Burschell and Listokin, 1978).

3. See Wilkinson (1974) for an analysis of how decisions that tend to reduce the complexity of interaction among residents and their local businesses contribute to an overall decline in the quality of life.

4. For reviews of energy and boomtown studies see Carley and Bustelo, 1984.

5. For sample checklists see Finsterbusch and Wolf, 1977, and the Interorganizational Committee on Guidelines and Principles for Social Impact Assessment, 1994.

6. The approach where all community factors are presented for discussion among affected groups contrasts with benefit/cost analysis that reduces complexity to a net numerical value (Finsterbusch, 1980; Watkins, 1980).

7. "Applied anthropology concepts and methodology, which facilitate direct observation of a population within its environment, function to articulate the social with the physical elements of a plan. In doing so, human behavior

patterns and felt needs can be related to the physical environment, land use and architectural design and can thus improve the overall quality of urban planning" (Nakajima, 1979, p. 5).

8. For references on developing social indicators see Wolf, 1979; Carley and Bustelo, 1984 and UNESCO, 1981.

9. For applications of SIA to urban and regional planning see Cramer, Dietz and Johnston, 1980; Rohe, 1982; De'Ath, 1982 in addition to the anthologies listed in references.

10. For the incorporation of social issues into physical plan elements in Cleveland see Krumholz, 1982, and for a report on the Boulder, Colorado experience see Cramer, Dietz and Johnston, 1980.

11. Most of the 19 Rio Grande Indian Pueblos maintain a traditional form of government, with officials such as the Governor being appointed by religious officials to serve the community voluntarily for one or two years. Accumulation of personal power is discouraged.

12. Two tools an ethnographer might use in SIA to anticipate people's response to a change are time allocation analysis and decision analysis.

13. Where an impact causes the quality of life to improve for some people and to decline for others, the distribution of impacts should be fully reported in an SIA, not "averaged out" or aggregated into net impact (Johnston, 1977).

REFERENCES

Armour, A., B. Bowran, E. Miller and M. Miloff. 1977. "A Framework for Community Impact Assessment" in K. Finsterbusch and C.P. ed. *Methodology of Social Impact Assessment*. New York: McGraw-Hill.

Burschell, R., and D. Listokin. 1978. *The Fiscal Impact Handbook*. New Brunswick, N.J. : Rutgers University Center for Urban Planning Research.

Canan, P. and M. Hennessey. 1982. "Community Values as the Context for Interpreting Social Impacts" in *Environmental Impact Review*, Vol. 3, 4: 351-365.

Carley, M.J. and E.S. Bustelo. 1984. *Social Impact Assessment and Monitoring*. Boulder and London: Westview Press.

Cramer, J. T. Dietz and R. Johnston. 1980. "Social Impact Assessment of Regional Plans: A Review of Methods and Issues and a Recommended Process" in *Policy Sciences*, Vol. 12: 61-82.

D'Ath, C. "Social Impact Assessment: A Critical Tool in Land Development Planning" in *International Social Science Journal*, vol. 34, 3: 441-450.

Duncan and Jones. 1976. *Methodology and Guidelines for Assessing Social Impacts of Development*. Berkeley, Calif.: Duncan and Jones Inc.

Finsterbusch, K. 1977. *Methodology of Social Impact Assessment*. New York: McGraw Hill.

_____ 1980. *Understanding Social Impacts: Assessing the Effects of Public Projects*. Beverly Hills and London: Sage Publications.

Geisler, C.C., R. Green, D. Usner and P. West. 1982. *Indian SIA: The Social Impact Assessment of Rapid Resource Development on Native Peoples*. Monograph No. 3. Ann Arbor, Mich.: University of Michigan, Natural Resources Sociology Research Lab.

Hill, M. 1968. "A Goals Achievement Matrix for Evaluating Alternative Plans" in *Journal of the American Institute of Planners*, Vol. 34: 19-28.

Howe, B. 1988. "Social Aspects of Physical Planning" in F.S. So and J. Getzels ed. *The Practice of Local Government Planning*. Washington D.C.: International City Management Association.

Hustedde, R., R. Shaffer and G. Pulver. 1988. *Community Economic Analysis: A How To Manual.* Ames, Iowa: Iowa State University North Central Regional Center for Rural Development.

Intergovernmental Committee on Guidelines and Principles for Social Impact Assessment. 1994. *Guidelines and Principles for Social Impact Assessment.* NOAA Technical Memorandum NMFS-f/SPO-16. U.S. Department of Commerce, National Oceanic and Atmospheric Administration and National Marine Fisheries Service.

Johnston, R.A. 1977. "The Organization of Social Impact Information for Use by Decision Makers and Citizens" in J. McEvoy and T. Dietz etc. *Handbook for Environmental Planning.* New York: Wiley Interscience.

Krumholz, N. 1982. "Equity and Economic Development" in A. L. Schorr ed. *Cleveland Development: A Dissenting View.* Cleveland Ohio: David Press.

Lapping M.B., T.L. Daniels and J.W. Keller. 1989. *Rural Planning & Development in the United States.* New York: Guilford Hall.

Lauber, D. 1976. "Socially Informed Planning and Decision Making: Some Preliminary Ideas" in Bureau of Urban and Regional Planning Research. *Intergovernmental Planning, Approaches to the "No Growth" vs. "Growth Is Good" Dilemma.* Urbana-Champaign, Illinois: University of Illinois.

Leistriz, F.L. and B. Ekstrom 1986. *Social Impact Assessment and Management: An Annotated Bibliography.* New York and London: Garland Publishing.

Lichfield, N. and Kettle. 1975. *Evaluation in the Planning Process.* Oxford: Pergamon.

Meredith, T.C. 1992. "Environmental Impact Assessment, Cultural Diversity and Sustainable Rural Development" in *Environmental Impact Assessment Review,* Vol. 12, Nos. 1,2: 125-138.

Nakajima, W.N. 1979. "From Census Tract to Neighborhood Planning" in *Practicing Anthropology: Special Section, Anthropology and Planning,* Vol. 1, Nos. 5/6: 5, 25,26.

Partridge, W.L. ed. 1984. *Training Manual in Development Anthropology,* Publication No. 17. Washington D.C.: American Anthropological Association and Society for Applied Anthropology.

Pelto, P.J. and G.H. Pelto. 1970. *Anthropological Research: The Structure of Inquiry.* Cambridge: Cambridge University Press.

Pinel, S.L. 1979. "Tradition as Innovation in Rural Development Planning." Thesis for M.S. in Urban and Regional Planning, University of Wisconsin: Madison.

_____ 1988. "Stopping the Flood of Damages from Cochiti Dam." *The Cultural Survival Quarterly*, vol. 12, 2: 21-24.

_____ 1991. "A Community Planning Approach to Resource Protection and Development," unpublished paper. Santa Fe, N.M.

Pollak, P.B. and A.N. Gorman. 1989. *Community Based Housing for the Elderly.* No. 420. Washington D.C.: American Planning Association, Planning Advisory Service.

Redfield, R. 1941. *Folk Cultures of the Yucatan.* Chicago: University of Chicago Press.

Ritzdorf, M. 1987. "Planning and the Intergenerational Community: Balancing the Needs of the Young and the Old in American Communities" in *Journal of Urban Affairs*, Vol. 9, No.1: 79-89.

Rohe, W.M. 1982. "Social Impact Analysis and the Planning Process in the United States: A Review and Critique" in *Town Planning Review*, Vol. 53, No. 4: 367-382.

Schlotter, J. and S.L. Pinel. 1992. "Anthropological Methods for Regional Planners." Workshop. Given at the Annual Conference of the Society for Applied Anthropology, Memphis, Tenn.

So, F.S. 1988. "Planning Agency Management" in So and Getzels eds. *The Practice of Local Government Planning.* Washington D.C.: ICMA.

Stanley, R., and Rattray. 1978. "Social Severance" in N.W. Pierce ed. *The Valuation of Social Cost.* London: George Allen and Unwin.

Stea, D. and C. Buge. 1982. "Cultural Impact Assessment on Native American Reservations: Two Case Studies" in Geisler, Green, Usner, and West eds. *Indian SIA: The Social Impact Assessment of Rapid Resource Development on Native Peoples*, No. 3. Ann Arbor Mich.: University of Michigan Natural Resources Sociology Research Lab.

Stoffle R. et al. 1990. "Holistic Conservation and Cultural Triage." *Human Organization*, vol. 49, No. 2: 91-99.

United Nations Educational, Scientific, and Cultural Organization. *Socio-economic Indicators for Planning: Methodological Aspects and Selected Examples,* No 2. Paris: UNESCO.

Vlachos, E. 1977. "The Use of Scenarios for Social Impact Assessment" in K. Finsterbusch and C.P. Wolf eds. *Methodology of Social Impact Assessment.* New York: McGraw Hill.

Vlachos, E. 1982. "Cumulative Impact Assessment" in *Impact Assessment Bulletin* No. 4: 60-70.

Watkins, G.C. and J. Fong. 1980. "Comparisons in Economic Development: Alberta and Texas" in *Journal of Energy and Development,* Vol. 6, No. 1: 1-24.

Wilkinson, K.P. 1974. "Consequences of Decline and Social Adjustment to It" in L.R. Whiting ed. *Communities Left Behind: Alternatives for Development.* Ames, Iowa: Iowa State University Press.

Wolf, C.P. 1979. *Quality of Life, Concept and Measurement: A Preliminary Bibliography.* Vance Bibliographies.

Sandra Lee Pinel is currently a Senior Planner for Intergovernmental Programs at the State of New Mexico Local Government Division, where she is responsible for working with the regional planning districts and state agencies to streamline local assistance programs and to develop a planning program. Previously she directed programs of integrated social and economic development for Native American tribes and organizations. Pinel is a member of the Society for Applied Anthropology and has published and spoken on the topic of culturally appropriate planning methods.

Urban Education:
Issues, Reforms,
and the Role of Planners

By Jerome L. Kaufman, AICP, and Kenneth C. Newman

Historically, urban planners have played a minor role in the planning of public schools, unlike their major roles in land use, transportation, housing, and recreation planning, and the increasingly important role they are now playing in economic development planning. Their involvement in planning for schools has been limited mainly to providing advice about location and size of school facilities and forecasting future school enrollments.

The reasons city planners have been minor players in urban education affairs stem partly from their disciplinary emphasis and partly from political realism. Because city planning's emphasis has been traditionally on urban space and the physical environment, interest in what goes on *within* urban school systems (e.g., governance, management, curriculum and service issues) has always been a low priority concern of city planners.

But, more importantly, even if urban planners wanted to play a larger role, their limited access to those who make educational policy keeps them out of that decision-making loop. Semi-autonomous school boards, not local governments, are responsible for setting urban school policies and priorities. Because city planners work for local government, they follow directives and priorities emanating principally from the offices of mayors, city councils, and planning commissions. They are not connected institutionally to the offices of school boards.

Education and City Goals

This paper's premise is that city planners need to become more active in the urban education arena. Despite their limited involvement in urban education affairs in the past, planners need to become *more informed* about a wide range of contemporary educational programs being discussed and debated that are aimed at improving the quality of urban education. With such knowledge, they can be better positioned to become *more involved and perhaps more influential players* in the urban education arena in the cities and metropolitan areas they serve. Why is this important? Because what is and will be happening to urban schools in the 1990s and into the next century will be critically important in determining whether cities will be able to achieve some critical goals (e.g., fiscal health, a trained work force for central-city and metropolitan-area employers, crime reduction, neighborhood revitalization, improved race relations, and retention of the middle class). These are also goals which urban planners obviously want to see achieved. More specifically, how do public school systems affect the capacity of cities to achieve these goals?

Fiscal. Most cities are heavily dependent on property taxes to pay for city services. Because about one-half of the property taxes that central-city residents pay goes for public schools, the capacity of city governments to fund their other expenditures is clearly dependent on the level of school expenditures. One has only to think back to the passage of Propositions 13 in California and 2 and 1/2 in Massachusetts in the 1970s, which started the rush towards capping property tax increases—as of 1987, 43 states had imposed property tax limitations (Ornstein 1988)—to realize that the steep rise in school spending contributes significantly to the cities' fiscal troubles. Another factor affecting a city's fiscal condition relates to its demographics. As the number of elderly, traditionally the age group least supportive of increased funding for schools, continues to increase as a percentage of total population in most older cities, local officials cannot expect the same political and financial support for education as in the past.

Crime. Some experts contend that the increased prison population stems largely from the failure of the urban education system. Lack of education has been shown to be a characteristic of many who move into criminal activity. The Correctional Education Association, a group of educators who work in prisons, estimates that only one in four prisoners has a high school diploma. One recent study done in Maryland prisons found that 93 percent of the prisoners scored below the 8th grade level in reading, which signifies functional illiteracy (*New York Times* 1991).

Unemployment and marginal employment. Demographic projections make it clear that, over the next 20 years, the American economy will depend increasingly on a work force drawn from minority groups, many of them living in the inner cities. Clearly, those central-city youngsters who lack basic educational skills will be ill prepared to compete for the better-paying central-city and suburban jobs. More likely, they will become either marginally employed, unemployed, or discouraged workers, with some ending up as criminals. Because those hired for marginal jobs will obviously earn less, their economic vulnerability could make them candidates at some later time for the city's growing dependent population.

Neighborhood development. Efforts to improve and revitalize neighborhoods are affected by school board decisions to close schools, especially when the closings are in more fragile, inner-city neighborhoods. Some schools also, because of budgetary constraints or school board policy, may have to shut their doors to the larger community surrounding them. More neighborhood instability, hastening the decline of some more vulnerable neighborhoods, could result.

Race relations. Schools are also a factor in how ethnic and racial groups get along in the city. The success or failure of school integration efforts can have an important effect on race relations in the community.

The middle class. Many studies have shown that one of the most important reasons middle class people leave the central cities is because they perceive that the quality of public education has declined to the point that they no longer want to send their children to public schools where the majority of children come from disadvantaged homes. The loss of middle class people contributes to a host of problems, among them: neighborhood decline, fewer residents with the economic means to buy goods and services to support central-city businesses, and less local tax revenue.

Given the significance of the public school system in affecting economic, fiscal, and social conditions in cities, it behooves planners to become more active and involved in the urban education arena. This paper will first highlight several key indicators of contemporary urban education problems. It will then discuss a number of current approaches aimed at improving the quality of urban education that planners should know more about. Special attention will be given to educational programs that address the needs of the most difficult group of students to educate—disadvantaged children living in the most problem-ridden areas of the city. Finally, it will offer some suggestions about how planners can become more active and potentially influential players in the urban education sphere.

Urban Education in Trouble—The Indicators

Many central-city school systems are in trouble. Some are in deep trouble, facing what amounts to a crisis in legitimacy. Problems in urban education are generating more discussion and debate than ever before about which paths to follow in trying to improve the quality of public schools. Although opinions differ about solutions to the urban education conundrum, most experts would concur that the following characteristics give rise to concern.

Minority-dominated urban schools. In 1984, minority children accounted for almost three-fourths of the students in the 37 largest urban school districts (Council of Great City Schools 1987). The percentage of minority students in urban school districts continues to climb. Statistics clearly show this pattern for selected cities. In 1990, for example, the following school districts across the country had 75 percent or more minority students: Phoenix, Chicago, Baltimore, Atlanta, Boston, San Antonio, Los Angeles, New York City, Miami, Hartford, Dallas, Oakland and Kansas City. It is also clear that more and more cities with a smaller minority population as a percentage of their total population, are experiencing steeper rises in the number of minority children in their public schools (e.g., in 1990, Minneapolis had a minority population of 22 percent but 44 percent of its public school students were minority).

High dropout rate. A key indicator often used to assess the quality of schools is the high school drop out rate. A very large number of youth—from 40 to 45 percent—in cities like Boston, Los Angeles, Baltimore, Milwaukee, and Chicago are high school dropouts. These rates vary considerably within a school district. The Chicago Panel on Public School Policy and Finance, for example, found that in one third of the city's 60 high schools, the dropout rate was 25 percent; in another third of the high schools, the dropout rate was almost 60 percent (Chicago Panel on Public School Policy 1987).

Low test scores. Another key indicator of educational quality is student performance on standardized tests. Here too, urban schools fare more poorly. The majority of students in big city public schools drop behind the national average in reading after the fourth grade and never catch up (Hill 1992). In the well-known report, "An Imperiled Generation: Saving Urban Schools" (1988), the Carnegie Foundation for the Advancement of Teaching noted the following about high schools in selected urban communities: the average high school senior in New Orleans was reading at a level exceeded by 80 percent of the students in the country; only five of Chicago's high schools had averages approaching national reading norms; two of every five students in Boston's high schools who reached the senior grade level (44 percent of this city's high school students were already dropouts) scored below the 30th percentile on a standardized reading test. "They may graduate," the report concluded, "but they are functionally illiterate."

Unsafe schools. Incidences of violence in and around schools are on the rise. A recent Harris poll of 96 schools across the country found that 40 percent of the central-city students said they know someone personally who had been killed or injured by gunfire (Chira 1993). The image of the Paterson, New Jersey, high school principal, Joe Clark, maintaining order by walking through the school's halls with a baseball bat in hand, is one well known to many. Although most would disagree with such a drastic approach to keeping urban schools safe, the issue of school safety for children as well as for teachers has become more prominent.

Other indicators. Urban school districts also tend to have other problems: higher rates of student absentees (in some states districts with higher absentee rates receive less state aid because state funding for education is tied to school attendance rates); higher student mobility rates (excessive mobility—i.e., a change of schools by students within the same school district during the school year—is more prevalent in inner-city areas and leads to lower student achievement); higher student retention rates (these are students who get left back more frequently instead of moving on to the next grade level); lower teacher morale; and more obsolete school facilities.

Approaches to Improving Urban Education

A wide range of educational strategies is being put forth to address urban education problems. Some are juxtaposed against others. For example, proponents of school choice sometimes line up on the opposite side of proponents of the effective schools movement. Those favoring school integration are being challenged by some who want separate schools or separate classes for minority students with curriculums more centered on the culture and achievements of that particular group. Most agree that big centralized school district bureaucracies need to be scaled down in size with their power decentralized. Disagreements arise, however, over the nature of the decentralized system. How much authority should principals have in setting policy for the specific school versus teachers? And what should be the roles of parents and community representatives in school governance? Debates are also taking place over whether some public school funds should go to private and religious schools to help in the effort to educate needier students. Still others disagree about whether suburbs have a responsibility to assist central-city school systems. Should states step in more vigorously to reduce per-pupil funding disparities between suburban and central-city school districts? should schools be desegregated throughout the metropolitan area so that central-city children can go to suburban schools?

School-based management. Large urban school systems have been targeted by many as examples of centralized, bureaucratic, and ineffective governments that stifle progress. The harshest critics see such districts as giant money traps, consuming half of the property taxes while keeping administrators out of touch and teachers counting their days to retirement.

To some, the solution is to transfer power from the central school administration to the individual schools, giving more authority to make decisions for the school to members of a school-based committee. Known as school- or site-based management, the notion is that schools work best when the principal, teachers, and parents share a common purpose, work together, and have the opportunity to unleash their untapped creativity.

Most educational experts would agree that individual schools need more autonomy in making policy decisions. Disagreements arise over the extent of autonomy the individual school should have and the division of responsibility. Many political leaders (especially in Chicago)

School-based Management at Work

School-based management is a popular reform that has been carried out in a number of communities. The Miami-Dade County school system, led by Joseph Fernandez, who left in 1990 to become New York City's Superintendent of Schools, is one of the most publicized districts to follow this approach. Each of the 160 schools in the Miami program has its own budget and a management committee composed of the principal, teachers and parents; the school management committee makes most major decisions on matters from how many teachers should teach a certain subject to how long to keep the schools open after classes end. Rochester, Los Angeles, and New York City are some of the more well known of the many cities using this approach.

The most daunting attempt at school based management is taking place in Chicago. It came about because of two events: then Secretary of Education William Bennett's gloomy report on the district in "A Nation at Risk" (National Commission on Excellence in Education 1983), which branded its schools as the nation's worst, and the Chicago teachers strike of 1987.

A broad-based coalition prompted the state legislature to pass a law that called for a 25 percent cut of the school bureaucracy and the wholesale decentralization of most education decision making to the school building level, vesting the preponderance of authority in laymen rather than professionals. Six parents, two community representatives, two teachers, and the school principal make up the 11-member elected local school council (LSC) in each of Chicago's 540 public schools. The LSCs are responsible for developing an annual school improvement plan, setting the school's goals and agenda, and approving or rejecting the principal's budget. For teachers and principals, tenure has been replaced with four-year performance-based contracts. The LSC has the ability to terminate the employment of any school staff, including teachers and the principal. Early opposition to the plan was especially vociferous from the school principals. The Chicago reform, now in its third year, has seen some schools soar with newfound freedom to design programs and select teachers, but overall systemwide achievement test scores have declined (*Chicago Sun-Times* 1993).

claim this is the only way for large districts to survive in the future. Parents know the needs of their children and should be directly involved. School-based management is also seen as a way to better scrutinize the budget of schools since many now see too many central office administrators as costly and wasteful.

Opponents of this type of reform question the expertise and the ability of parents, who have little professional training in educational policies. Some picture the schools spinning out of control, as impatient parents pull the plug on attempts to improve schools that fail to show huge immediate gains.

One potential ripple effect is the creation of a climate of distrust among school personnel, parents, and politicians. In Chicago, local school council members complained that the central office was slow to begin training programs and just difficult to work with. Miami and Los Angeles have had similar problems smoothing the transition. Imposing a reform like school-based management on a large urban school system is a huge undertaking; the playing field can be filled with land mines.

A variation on the school-based management approach is when an urban school board hires an outside group to manage some or all of its schools. One reason to do so is to tap experts outside the local educational establishment who have fresh ideas about managing troubled schools.

A few colleges are beginning to provide management services to troubled school districts. The most well known example is Boston University, which took over the Chelsea, Massachusetts, school district in 1988 for a five-year period. Chelsea schools were failing by every measure; they had the highest dropout rates in the state and were among the schools with the lowest test scores. Boston University's Dean of Education is supervising the overhauling of Chelsea's five schools. Different arms of the university are being used in this endeavor. For example, faculty from the College of Liberal Arts are revising the curriculum, people from the Social Work School are helping new mothers prepare their children for school, and the School of Management is helping design Chelsea school budgets. A major portion of resources is being devoted to early childhood education and preschool programs. So far, the results are not encouraging as dropout and student absentee rates remain high, although test scores are mixed—i.e., some improvements but some declines as well (Shanker 1992).

SCHOOL CHOICE

The most widely discussed and debated educational reform of the 1980s is school choice. The term "choice" covers a wide range: public school plans that allow choice within school districts, between districts, or even statewide; public/private choice approaches like charter schools; and choice plans in which public funds in the form of vouchers are used to subsidize private school education. The common element of choice programs is that parents have a greater degree of freedom to select schools for their children. By giving parents the right, as it were, to take their business elsewhere, the idea was that public schools would become more accountable and thus better.

Proponents of choice (Chubb and Moe 1990, Finn 1991) see several benefits: better educational outcomes because competition among schools as a result of choice would lead to incentives for schools to improve themselves, to innovate more, to improve student achievement, and to control costs; parents would become more invested in the schools where they choose to send their children; and poor children would get a better education because they would have more options for schooling than just being limited to their own problem-ridden neighborhood schools. Under choice, the best schools are seen as retaining students and funding while schools that do not improve are seen as losing students and more likely to fail. In the context of central cities, school choice is seen as a way of keeping more middle class families from moving to the suburbs to escape what they perceive to be the city's low-quality public schools.

Critics of choice contend that choice is no panacea. They see it leading to educational inequalities because it lets parents with the most aggressive, driving instincts select the best schools for their children and leaves the rest of the children, especially poor children, in places nobody else wants to be (Kozol 1991, Greider 1992, Lemann 1991). Instead of breaking down stratification between wealthier and poorer schools, some critics contend that school choice solidifies it.

One recent study by the Carnegie Foundation for the Advancement of Teaching seems to support those skeptical of the claims of school choice proponents. The study concluded that choice programs primarily benefit children of better-educated parents, that choice programs do not necessarily lead to improved student performance, and without certain safeguards such programs might widen the gap between rich and poor school districts (*New York Times* 10/26/92).

Following is a review of some of the more widely discussed school choice plans.

Public School Choice

Intradistrict choice. School choice within school district boundaries is becoming more common across the country. Some districts allow such choice for special needs and programs. Other districts try to accommodate parent interest in different kinds of programs.

Beginning in the 1970s, many cities created choice plans to minimize forced busing. *Magnet schools* were a key response. In magnet school plans—which can include elementary, middle, and high schools—the district usually chooses a specific curricular theme or teaching method for the school and seeks to draw a student body from a larger attendance area, perhaps even from the entire city. Magnet school foci vary widely: schools for the gifted and talented, science and mathematics, college preparatory, the performing arts, languages, health care training, business and back-to-basics are among the possibilities. A study of 15 urban school districts showed that in 13 of them the number of

---

School Choice in Spanish East Harlem

District 4 in New York City's Spanish East Harlem is often heralded as a model for inner-city choice programs. In the mid-1970s, District 4 began allowing parents to choose the elementary and junior high schools their children would attend. Teachers were encouraged to create alternative schools using different teaching methods and curriculums. The district now has over 50 schools in 20 buildings. Class sizes have been reduced. Student achievement scores have risen. And most of the students who graduate from District 4 go on to finish high school.

---

magnet schools and students rose significantly from 1982-83 to 1988-89. By 1989, in cities like Buffalo, Cincinnati, St. Paul, San Diego, and Seattle, the total magnet school enrollment comprised one-third or more of the total student enrollment (Blank 1989).

In *controlled choice*, a variant of intradistrict choice, the district promotes parent choice but controls for racial balance. Among the 14 school districts in the country that operate with controlled choice (Walters 1991). Boston is one of the best known examples. In 1989, Boston created three zones in the city for elementary and middle schools.

Parents can choose schools within their zones, as long as those choices result in a rough racial balance both within the zone and in individual schools. School officials say that, for grades one through six, 80 percent of the children were able to enroll in the first school on their list (Daniels 1989).

A highly specific form of school choice is emerging in a number of cities—specialized public schools for African-American and Hispanic youth. The proponents see such schools as preserving racial identity, infusing children with racial pride, offering successful minority adult role models for the children, and raising their self esteem. Examples include: the Ujamaa Institute in New York City, a high school to be opened in the fall of 1993 aimed at black and Hispanic males, which will emphasize values and the cultures of blacks and Hispanics; six elementary schools in Detroit (the first three created in 1991 as educational alternatives for at-risk urban black boys by court order are now opened to girls as well) which teach an African-centered curriculum emphasizing black achievements; and schools with similar curriculums in Milwaukee, Baltimore, Minneapolis, Portland, Oregon, Camden, and a half a dozen other cities. Critics say such schools are subverting an ideal of a common culture by substituting ethnic pride. Defenders challenge this view. They contend that radical steps are needed because the public schools' record in educating minorities is so abysmal (Chira 1993).

Interdistrict choice. In these programs, students can attend a public school in another school district. Although many states are changing state laws governing school attendance, interdistrict choice is still relatively uncommon because most states still base aid to school districts on the number of students in attendance. Thus school districts try to keep their own students.

Interdistrict choice plans emerged largely in response to law suits or threatened law suits from inner-city minority parents who contended that suburban schools were segregated. In metropolitan areas like St. Louis, Kansas City, and Milwaukee, for example, voluntary school desegregation plans were created in which inner-city children were allowed to attend suburban schools and vice-versa.

One of the criticisms of voluntary desegregation programs is that inner-city students who are more motivated to learn leave the city for the suburban schools, thus leaving a higher proportion of problem students in the beleaguered inner-city schools. Benefits are seen, however, for the inner city students that transfer. A study of a voluntary busing program called Project Concern, which operated in the Hartford area for 20 years and which currently involves about 750 inner city minority students attending suburban schools, found strong long-term benefits of suburban attendance for inner city black students: lower dropout rates, higher chances of enrollment and success in college, and increased likelihood of living in an integrated as opposed to a segregated neighborhood as an adult (Orfield 1988).

Milwaukee's Interdistrict Choice Program

Milwaukee began an interdistrict choice program, Chapter 220, in 1983. In 1991, about 4,500 Milwaukee students transferred to suburban schools, while about 1,000 suburban students came into Milwaukee public schools, most to attend Milwaukee's magnet or specialty schools. Under an appellate court order in 1990, more than a fourth of Kansas City's black students could transfer to predominantly white schools in the suburbs at the state's expense.

Statewide choice. In 1988, Minnesota adopted the nation's first statewide choice plan. Since then, seven other states adopted some form of statewide choice (Walters 1991). The Minnesota plan provides state aid for any transferring students to go to the receiving school district. They, in turn, have the right to accept or reject incoming students, although rejection on racial grounds is prohibited. Only 3,220 Minnesota students in 1989 (less than one percent of all students in Minnesota schools), however, chose to attend schools outside their home districts (Witte 1990). The Minnesota plan also allows high school students to take college courses if such courses are unavailable in their schools, again with a transfer of state aid.

A controversy arising from statewide choice recently occurred in Des Moines. Iowa is one of the eight states that allows statewide choice. In 1992, the Des Moines school board, concerned about a disproportionate number of requests from white families in Des Moines to send their children to other districts, voted to reject all 122 petitions by white students to transfer while accepting the six made by minority children. Its decision was challenged in court as an example of reverse discrimination. The case offers an extreme illustration of the problems an urban school district can encounter (although Des Moines's schools have only 20 percent minority children) as it tries to maintain racial balance while providing a state-mandated escape valve (Wilkerson 1992).

Public/Private School Choice

Charter schools. Most proponents of school choice see the choice approach played out essentially in public school districts. Some prefer that schools of choice be outside public authority in private schools. The *charter school* idea—first enacted in Minnesota in 1991, adopted by the California legislature in 1992, and being considered in Wisconsin, New Jersey, and several other states, as well as in Detroit, Chicago, Philadelphia, Baltimore, and Milwaukee—provides the opportunity for change-oriented educators to go either to the local school district or to some other public body for a contract under which they would set up an autonomous (and therefore outcome-based) school that children could choose to attend without charge (Kolderie 1992).

Charter schools must observe health and safety codes and meet the requirements that essentially define public education (e.g., nondiscrimination, no charging of tuition, giving everyone an equal chance of being admitted, no religious character to the school). Beyond these standards, charter schools, in exchange for agreeing to testing student performance, are independent of central administration and free to decide for themselves.

The school's existence depends on its meeting the student performance objectives it agreed with its sponsor it would meet. Minnesota charter school proposals are diverse (e.g., schools propose to specialize in a particular learning method, in a subject field, in at-risk children, or for children of a particular age group). Four schools have been chartered, with only one so far operating. This is St. Paul's City Academy, with four teachers, two aides, and two psychologists serving 35 students of high school age who have a history or truancy or other disciplinary problems.

Because charter schools are to receive the average per-pupil amount spent in Minnesota and allow licensed teachers to run innovative new programs free from most state mandates, opposition to them has arisen from teachers unions and statewide education associations. The jury is still out on whether charter schools will succeed, but interest in them as an optional form of choice for parents appears to be high.

Private School Choice

Vouchers. First proposed by conservative economist Milton Freidman in the late 1950s, voucher plans aim to create a "free market" for educational services. In the most radical proposals, government would issue each family a check or voucher representing the government's per-student educational expenditure. Families would then be free to choose any school for their children and to add to the value of the voucher from their own resources.

Private schools, in some schemes even religious schools, would be eligible under this arrangement. Many saw the original voucher idea as a subsidy for the middle and upper classes who could more easily add value to that of a voucher. Some voucher proponents have developed plans to try to blunt this and other equity concerns. For example, all schools would be required to accept a certain percentage of low-income and at-risk students, supplemental fees would be limited, and strict prohibitions on selective choice by race would be enforced (Coon and Sugarman 1978).

A modest voucher program proposed by an African-American Democrat state legislator from Milwaukee was adopted by the Wisconsin legislature in 1990. Called the Milwaukee Parental Choice Program, the program provided 970 low-income students from the Milwaukee public schools, one percent of the city's public school students, with state funds to attend private nonsectarian schools. Eight private schools agreed to accept the students, who take along $2,500 each in state aid that would have gone to the Milwaukee public schools. It is interesting that the original bill proposed by Wisconsin's Republican Governor in 1987 included parochial schools (Wells 1990).

BUSINESS COMMUNITY INVOLVEMENT IN SCHOOLS

Corporate America, aware that half of first-time job seekers through the 1990s will be minorities, has become increasingly concerned about the quality of the urban education system and its role in improving it. Because many business leaders recognize that the competency of the future work force relies heavily on the public school system, corporate activism on behalf of improving public schools is on the rise.

Boston launched the first business-school compact in 1982. Today, corporate groups in more than 20 cities have done likewise. In addition, big corporations like Pepsi Cola, Citibank, Nabisco, IBM, and General Electric have spent millions of dollars in assisting public schools. The efforts of the business community cover a wide range of add-on activities that augment what the schools are doing. These include:

- *Donating or loaning resources to schools.* This could be in the form of mentors for school children (about 150 of Cincinnati's Procter and Gamble's employees serve as mentors to students in an inner city high school) or support staff and consultants to school officials. Companies also donate material things to schools like computers and science lab equipment.

- *Offering incentives and rewards to students.* In Cleveland, for example, the business community underwrites a "scholarship in escrow" for pupils in grades 7-12. Students earn $40 per A, $20 per B, and $10 per C to apply toward college training. Other money-for-grades approaches are operative in Dallas, Detroit, and Kansas City schools, although some educators criticize this approach as a quick fix for a problem requiring more serious attention.

- *Guaranteeing jobs, college entry, or financial aid for successful high school graduates.* The Baltimore Commonwealth, one such business alliance, launched a priority hiring program in 1985 where private employers would hire public school graduates with a 95 percent attendance rate and a grade point average of 80. They were guaranteed three job interviews from a pool of 150 participating employers (Steinbach 1988). The Detroit Compact signs agreements with 6th graders in which they pledge to maintain a C average and at least a 90 percent attendance record. In return, a job or college scholarship would await them when they graduate high school.

Overall, the scale of corporate investment in public education is modest. Robert Reich, now U.S. Secretary of Labor, said that from 1988-91 private corporations donated a total of $250 million to public schools, equivalent to the budget the New York City School district needs to operate for three months. Furthermore, only a small portion of all corporate donations to education—six percent in 1989—went to public primary or secondary schools (Folbre 1992).

Although the corporate community cannot solve the problems of urban education, many believe that because they recognize clearly that they have an important stake in improving the quality of urban education, they can play an important role in stimulating innovation and change in urban schools.

PRESCHOOL EDUCATION

In the past, urban education policy focused principally on what went on in the schools from kindergarten to 12th grade. Many now believe that urban education reforms will not succeed unless they incorporate ways of reaching inner-city children well before they enter kindergarten. Recognizing that malnutrition, neglect, and abuse can severely hinder a child's early brain development and therefore learning ability, early childhood education programs are seen as critical. The theory is that, if you want well-educated citizens and workers to emerge at the end of the school pipeline, you have to put healthy, happy, and motivated children into the system at the beginning. But this is especially difficult in poor families where pre-school children are often unprepared for school because of health or emotional problems or trouble at home.

The lead goal in the manifesto produced at the White House education summit meeting in 1989 read "By the year 2000, all children in America will start school ready to learn." Although political and philosophical differences arise about how children should be ready to learn, most would agree with the goal. Conservatives would emphasize the role of the family in getting children ready while liberals, accepting the family's role as important, would go further in calling for some government intervention especially for children from poor and disadvantaged families.

Some newer programs like New York City's Project Giant Step appear to be surpassing Head Start. Begun in 1986 to provide a comprehen-

The Head Start Story

The Head Start program, one of the few Great Society programs to continue to receive bipartisan support, is the most well known of the child readiness programs. More than a preschool program stressing cognitive and emotional learning, Head Start also provides its children with medical and dental care and access to healthy food. Some contend that Head Start's success stems from improvement of the noncognitive development of children, not their cognitive learning as reflected in good test scores. In fact, the evaluation studies of children in Head Start are inconclusive. Although educational deficiencies of the children appear to decrease in the short term, the long-term effects of Head Start on academic preparedness are transitory (Finn 1991). Head Start is still limited because teachers are low paid, only the poorest families are eligible, and less than a third of the Head Start programs are located in public schools, making the transition to public school for children more difficult.

sive public preschool program for children of low-income families, Project Giant Step, with 280 classes in the city, has gained many adherents. The first study of the effect of Giant Step showed that this half-day program had more than twice the positive impact on children's performance on cognitive tests as Head Start and other early childhood programs (Wells 1990). The study also showed that Giant Step children had large gains in social and emotional development. By adding more staff and more staff training, having an intensive support program for the parents, and linking the city's public schools with the city's social service agency for child development in administering the program, Project Giant Step builds on and improves Head Start.

MORE FUNDING FOR URBAN SCHOOLS

In recent years, a number of legal challenges have been raised to school finance inequities. The central contention of these challenges, which has landed states like New Jersey, Kentucky, Texas and Connecticut in court, is that huge disparities exist between rich and poor school districts in per-pupil expenditures.

Perhaps the foremost critic of the funding inequity between rich and poor school districts is Jonathon Kozol, who documented huge disparities in spending between inner-city school systems with predominantly minority student populations in Chicago, Camden, East St. Louis,

Detroit, and San Antonio and their mostly white suburban counterparts (1991). More effective education, he contends, takes place in modern, well-maintained school buildings in suburbs with an abundance of science labs, computers, and the latest textbooks. He cited East St. Louis as a particularly egregious example where roofs on its schools routinely leak and raw sewage floats into some school buildings.

States have followed different paths to address the problems of inequities. The Kentucky state legislature passed a $500 million educational finance program that would dramatically increase state aid to poor districts and cap spending hikes in rich districts unless voters approve them. Governor Florio of New Jersey first proposed that 350 of the 611 school districts in the state share a $1 billion increase in state financing in 1991-92. Aid to the state's predominantly prosperous suburbs, however, would be cut 25 percent a year for four years starting in the 1992-93 academic year. Florio's plan, however, was strongly attacked, with almost half of the state aid proposed for poorer school districts being converted into a plan for property tax relief. The Texas legislature recently approved an amendment to its State Constitution shifting 2.75 percent of its current state budget, or $410 million, from school districts of high property wealth to poor ones (Verhovek 1993).

MAKING SCHOOLS MORE EFFECTIVE FOR INNER-CITY CHILDREN

Proponents of the several educational reforms discussed in this paper would probably each contend that children from disadvantaged homes in inner cities would probably receive a better education if the programs they favored were carried out. Those supporting school choice would say that the children of poor families would undoubtedly benefit because they will be able to go to better schools instead of being locked into low-quality schools in the poor neighborhoods in which they live. Backers of business-school partnerships would say that their incentive programs would encourage minority youth to stay in school and therefore get a better education. Supporters of school-based management would claim that the flexibility and innovation unleashed from shifting authority from the central school bureaucracy to the individual schools would lead to improved schooling for disadvantaged youths.

Proponents of school desegregation would argue that minority youth from poor families would benefit from their association with middle class children because they have stronger educational aspirations and study habits. And advocates of programs to equalize school funding between rich and poor school districts would contend that bringing poor districts up to parity with rich districts would lead to more resources for the poorer districts to use to raise the quality of education for their children. None of these educational reforms, however, say much about the kind of educational programs that children from disadvantaged backgrounds should receive in the schools they attend. In contrast, some reformers have focused on developing programs aimed at improving the quality of education for disadvantaged youth *within* the school building itself.

In the 1960s, James Coleman undertook a major study (1966), to determine whether inner-city schools were getting the same or fewer resources as other schools. In his classic study, Coleman concluded that unequal school resources were not the primary cause of inadequate education for the children of the urban poor. Rather, the most important determinants of learning for policy makers to consider were the influences of the youngster's home background—particularly family and neighborhood.

Coleman in effect provided the philosophical rationale for racial integration in the schools—busing inner-city children to schools with middle class children so that they would have contact with children from better home backgrounds. Magnet schools, choice programs, racially integrated schools are all approaches that aim at negating the effects of the "harmful" environment in which disadvantaged children live, by in effect getting them "out" of that environment.

Charles Payne (1987) contends, however, that Coleman asked the wrong question. Instead of asking Why are urban schools failing?, Payne says Coleman should have focused on the 55 schools in his sample that were effective in educating children from poor families by asking Why were some schools in problem-ridden neighborhoods successful? Although Payne acknowledges that poor home environments deter learning, he believes Coleman should have focused on why some inner-city schools did better than others.

The effective schools movement, pioneered by Roland Edmunds' studies of Detroit schools in the 1970s that he found to be effective, spawned work on developing a number of '"within-school" educational approaches. Edmunds' belief was that all children, including those from disadvantaged backgrounds, are "eminently educable" and that the behavior of the school is critical in determining the quality of that education. Edmunds, who focused on elementary schools in his research, emphasized the following principles for an effective school: strong leadership; high expectations for the children; an emphasis on basic skills, especially reading; an orderly climate; and careful monitoring of student progress.

James Comer, a Yale University child psychiatrist, extended Edmunds' work. He concentrated on the emotional, social, and psychological needs of inner-city children to negate the destructive social climate in which they live. Comer, whose approach is now being used by more than 100 schools around the country and whose efforts were rewarded by a five-year, $15 million grant from the Rockefeller Foundation in 1990, started his excursion into the labyrinth of inner-city education in New Haven in the late 1960s in two of that city's worst elementary schools. One school eventually dropped out of the program. The other, the King school, went on to become one of the country's most frequently cited cases of success in urban education. Ranking at the bottom of New Haven's 31 elementary schools in reading and math test scores in 1969, the King school, drawing from the same pool of poor minority children, jumped by 1979 to being in the top third of New Haven's schools in test score performance. In addition, student attendance ranked third best in the city, and parent attendance at school functions increased dramatically.

Comer's approach has three critical components—a governance team, that involves all the adult stakeholders in the school (principal, teachers, staff, parents, etc.) in sharing responsibility for managing the school; a parents program, which tries to involve as many parents as possible in the school's life—social activities, volunteer activities, and the work of the governance committee; and a mental health team, composed of a child psychologist, social worker, and guidance counselor, which encourages both teachers and parents to think about children in developmental terms and helps them find solutions to the problems of individual children. Comer also emphasizes several guidelines: a "no-fault" policy, which focuses on problem solving not blame fixing; consensus decision making; improving the social skills of the students by linking the curriculum to the larger community so that students become effective participants in society; and allowing principals to have authority while at the same time being responsive to all concerned parties (Payne 1991).

Henry Levin, of Stanford University, shares with Comer and Edmunds the notion that all children are educable. He emphasizes the nature of the curriculum in his approach more than Comer who focuses more on relationships and process. Levin adamantly opposes the idea that the best way to teach children from impoverished homes is to provide them with remedial help in math, reading and other basic subjects. "Once you begin to talk about kids needing remediation," he contends, "you're talking about damaged merchandise . . . you have lost the battle" (Wells 1989). Working in a San Francisco elementary school, with a third of its students being Hispanic from poor homes, his accelerated learning program emphasizes treating subjects in depth by, for example, relating them to students' everyday lives. The curriculum centers on a "whole language" approach to reading instruction that is used often with gifted students, but rarely with below-average ones. Students get introduced to more difficult words, for example, through use of poetry and books based on real life experiences. Children from different backgrounds and levels work together on projects whose success depends on how well the students cooperate and support each other. Levin's approach involves parent involvement, a curriculum that emphasizes higher-order thinking skills (including analysis and problem-solving), and goals that emphasize bringing all students up to grade level by the end of the school year. Reports indicate significant gains in test scores in the school.

Another well-known educational innovator, Theodore Sizer of Brown University, focused some of his attention on the beleaguered high schools in poor urban districts (1984). Sizer believes that the primary purpose of education is intellectual, to help students learn to use their minds well. His principles include: reducing the number of students for whom any high school teacher is responsible to no more than 80; concentrating on a few subjects in depth rather than glossing over many areas; eliminating the rigid 45-minute time slot for each class period; and replacing some standardized tests with demonstrated ability to carry out projects and assemble portfolios of work.

Although not aimed specifically at inner-city children, the approach of Howard Gardner in *The Unschooled Mind* (1991), offers a fresh perspective on educating children from disadvantaged backgrounds. Gardner takes issue with traditional educators who call for "basic skills," "cultural literacy," or the mandating of standardized tests. Schools, he argues, should be responsive to different forms of learning, performance, and understanding. His approach is premised on the belief that students are

School Size: A Factor in Better Education?

A growing consensus is emerging about another characteristic of urban high schools. A generation ago, educators endorsed large urban high schools because they could offer a wide range of subjects and extracurricular activities at a relatively low administrative cost. Now, however, many researchers and educators see big urban high schools as breeding grounds for dropouts, academic failure and alienation. The new view is that students in high schools limited to about 400 usually have fewer disciplinary problems, better attendance and graduation records, and sometimes higher grades and test scores. Philadelphia's system is the furthest along—the school district aims to create small high schools within all 22 of the city's large neighborhood high schools. So far, 15 of the high schools have been broken up into smaller subschools. Modest efforts in the direction of smaller high schools are also underway in New York City, Denver, San Francisco, Chicago, and Providence. Proponents of small high schools believe such schools need full autonomy, core curriculums with high standards, and a process by which students have to present what they learned in presentations to graduation committees before they receive their diplomas.

capable of at least seven different ways of "knowing the world," what he calls multiple intelligences—linguistic and logical-mathematical intelligences (which he contends are the intelligences primarily emphasized and tested for in schools today), and spatial, musical, bodily-kinesthetic, interpersonal, and intrapersonal intelligences.

His ideal educational environment for children would, in addition to their attending a formal school, allow them, starting at the age of seven or eight, to enroll in a children's museum, a science museum, or some kind of discovery center so that they could develop and use all their intelligences. He also envisions youngsters entering apprentice groups where they would have the opportunity to develop their literacies and artistic and kinesthetic talents, by having direct contact with adult experts in different disciplines.

Gardner discusses two practical applications of his educational philosophy. One is Project Spectrum, a classroom for pre-school children where each child's multiple intelligences are stimulated in different places in the classroom—a naturalist's corner, a story telling area, a building corner. The other is the Key School, an inner-city public elementary school in Indianapolis founded in the middle 1980s, where a child's multiple intelligences are designed to be stimulated each day. Three practices are pivotal. Each day each student participates in an apprenticeship-like pod, where the student works with peers of different ages and a competent teacher to master a craft or discipline of interest. Complementing the pods are strong ties to the community (e.g., a visit to the Indianapolis Children's Museum or a once a week visit from an outside specialist demonstrating an occupation or craft). Finally, each student has to prepare at least three projects during the year on specific school themes (e.g., Mexican Heritage, The Renaissance) in which they would present their projects to their classmates describing the project's genesis, purpose, problems, and future implications and draw on their multiple intelligences in doing so.

HOW PLANNERS CAN PLAY A MORE ACTIVE ROLE IN URBAN EDUCATION

This paper has attempted to make the case that the quality of a central city's public education system is critical to its future. Because of public education's prominence, the stakes are simply too high for urban planners to continue to play a limited role in the urban education field. They need to become more active players. What can they do?

We suggest three paths for planners:

1.   Become better informed about the issues, policies, and reforms currently being discussed, debated, and, in some instances, carried out in the urban education field.

2.   Incorporate more urban education thinking into planning instruments.

3.   Move more deliberately onto the urban education playing field.

The bulk of this paper travelled down the first path. It offered information about a variety of contemporary strategies in urban education, considering some of their strengths and weaknesses. Clearly, the more planners know about what's going on in the urban education policy arena, the greater is the chance that they can become more legitimate and influential players in that arena. The rest of this paper offers some

suggestions about what planners could do in travelling down the
second and third paths.

Injecting Urban Education Thinking into Planning

City plans. City plans are the most distinguishing products that planning agencies produce. When city planning reports address matters
dealing with the public education system, usually only a few issues are
covered. A case in point is the New York City Planning Commission's
recent report, *Shaping the City's Future*, which "articulates the City
Planning Commission's vision for New York's long-term future and
presents a preliminary set of planning and zoning policies to make the
vision a reality" (1993). Although most would agree that the public
schools are crucial to New York City's future, only two paragraphs of
this 133-page document deal with education. A need for "major improvements in public education . . . to give all New Yorkers, especially
the low-income, the knowledge and skills they require in today's
information-intensive economy," is stated, but the report is silent about
what these educational improvements should be. Instead, the planners
tread lightly on two familiar issues: the city's aging educational
physical plant (noting that the city plans to spend $7.4 billion over the
next 10 years to improve public facilities for education) and school
enrollment forecasts (recommending that the Planning Department
work with the Board of Education on developing better enrollment
forecasting models to determine long-term need for schools).

We see no reason why planning agencies must stay on the narrow turf.
They can address a wider range of educational issues in their planning
documents. At the least, city plans could call attention to how "critical"
public education is, noting its effects on a city's capacity to achieve
such important goals as fiscal health, a trained labor force for the city's
economy, neighborhood revitalization, crime reduction, improved race
relations, and retention of the middle class. It is indeed odd that city
plans, the public documents that most espouse comprehensiveness,
often fall short in recognizing the importance of the public education
system to cities.

Planning agencies can go further to incorporate more extensive urban
education thinking into their city plans. The recent Seattle comprehensive plan (Seattle Planning Department 1993) is a good example. In
a section called Seattle's Comprehensive Plan Framework Policies, a

product of city council actions involving hundreds of citizens over a two-year period, the import of public schools is clearly recognized.

The plan states that :

> Because schools are significant institutions for teaching youth and their families social skills, critical thinking and life-long learning, and because the quality of education is a critical factor in retaining households with children in the city . . . the City shall use all . . . resources at its disposal to ensure the development of pervasive excellence in education in the Seattle Public Schools . . .

The educational policies listed in the Seattle plan move far beyond the traditional school siting and size concerns of planners. They include:

- Improving the academic achievement of low-income students and students of color;

- Promoting multicultural education and cultural diversity;

- Preparing students for the types of jobs and work-places of the future;

- Encouraging parent and community involvement in schools;

- Advocating quality integrated education for all children;

- Ensuring that schools become integral parts of neighborhoods in which they are located;

- Encouraging parent and community involvement in schools;

- Promoting business investment of financial and human resources in the development of the public education system; and

- Ensuring that new schools and community facilities like parks and libraries are planned and sited in a coordinated fashion.

It is interesting that the above educational policies, apart from two that deal specifically with school capital facilities, are listed as falling "outside the scope of this Comprehensive Plan"; that is, they are not treated more fully in the plan report. Even though the Seattle planners conclude that most of the education policies fall outside their turf, their inclusion in the comprehensive plan document affords the plan greater salience and legitimacy in terms of the city's priorities.

School officials on planning committees. Planners could reach out more to the educational community by tapping more school officials to serve on planning committees and task forces. Putting highly regarded school district administrators, principals, or even teachers on citywide planning task forces (e.g., dealing with economic development, neighborhood revitalization, fiscal, affordable housing or fringe area development policy) would have several benefits. Not only would this acknowledge the closer link between public education and certain city planning policies, but it would also permit school officials to have more say on some important planning policies. By bringing education officials into more forums on citywide issues, it could lessen the "isolationism" of the public education community.

Clearly, another important linkage is at the neighborhood level. Schools are crucial facilities to be considered in most neighborhood planning efforts. Therefore, school officials need to be key members of neighborhood planning committees.

Education policy in neighborhood plans. Neighborhood plans, like city plans, often give short shrift to what's going on in the neighborhood's schools. These plans need to be more informative about the issues facing neighborhood schools and the ways in which the schools are dealing with them. An outstanding neighborhood planning effort is now underway in Baltimore's Sandtown-Winchester neighborhood in which the public schools are a cornerstone of the planning process (Rankin 1992).

Baltimore's Sandtown-Winchester neighborhood, one of the city's oldest neighborhoods with 12,000 people spread over 72 blocks has every social problem known to America's inner cities in abundance—44 percent of the labor force is unemployed, the median household income is less than $10,000 a year, 90 percent of the births are to unwed mothers, the neighborhood is one of the five highest crime areas in the city, and 75 percent of its housing stock is substandard.

A partnership effort is underway between neighborhood residents, city government, and private enterprise (Jim Rouse, who heads the Enterprise Foundation, is a key player). The aim is quite ambitious—to mount a comprehensive solution to overhaul community life. Started in February 1990 when Mayor Schmoke appointed a task force to guide the neighborhood's transformation, the Sandtown-Winchester planning effort is far-reaching in scope. It focuses on housing, health care, human services, employment assistance, commercial and retail development, community pride, parks and recreation areas, safety and security, and schools.

The program strategies for schools are premised on the notion that all students have the capacity to learn. A number of the reforms discussed in this report are reflected in the specific recommendations for public education in the Sandtown-Winchester neighborhood.

- Develop organizational culture and belief systems in each of the neighborhood's schools to deliver instructional programs that will ensure success of school improvement plans;

- Create parent centers that provide parent education, peer support, and opportunities for parent involvement in each school;

- Mount a comprehensive school readiness program to ensure that the neighborhood's children from birth through age five and their families receive services and support needed to prepare them for success in school;

- Initiate school-based strategic planning for each of the neighborhood's schools; the resulting school improvement plan must ensure that the following essential components of a successful education system—extended day programs, training and staff development, shared decision making, health and human service support, an outcome based core curriculum that meets state standards for attendance, promotion rates, and student achievement in reading, math, writing, social studies, and science;

- Offer professional incentives;

- Enhance the existing core programs in the neighborhood's three elementary schools (e.g. full-day kindergartens, a 1-to-12 adult-to-student ratio in all classrooms, extended-day program for students of parents who are employed, and free breakfast and lunch programs for students in need);

- Provide comprehensive student support services (registered nurse, mental health professional, social worker, guidance counselor in neighborhood schools to facilitate early intervention of health and human service problems to students and families);

- Institute the Next Generations program for eighth graders entering high school (each eighth grader would have an Academic Coach or Advocate to facilitate transition to high school, through high school, and from high school to work or to college);

- Ensure that each school will serve as a resource to neighborhood residents of all ages; strengthen ties between school and community and foster the use of the schools as a means of developing community pride, spirit and involvement; and

- Provide a smooth transition of authority and resources from the central office of the Baltimore City Public Schools to the neighborhood schools.

Getting Planners onto the Urban Education Playing Field

Planners as resource people in the schools. Planners have special talents that can be useful to public school teachers. They think about communities in comprehensive terms. They understand relationships among the different parts of a community. They are problem solvers who follow systematic ways of thinking in coming up with solutions to problems. And they have a special knowledge of a broad range of community issues, problems, approaches, and solutions. These qualities make them potentially valuable resource people for public school teachers at the elementary to high-school level to draw upon when they use the city and region as laboratories for learning for their students. One might even envision some city planning agencies taking a more proactive stance by informing the school board that some planning staff members are available as resource people in the classroom. Planning agencies might even begin to develop more tailored educational materials, with the help of urban educators, which the "planner-educators" might use in the schools. A side benefit of this role might be that school officials gain a better understanding of what urban planning is all about and how schools can help in solving the city's problems.

Planners as process and technical advisors to school officials. As noted above, one of the special talents of city planners is their problem-solving ability. In deriving solutions to problems, planners use processes like rational planning or strategic planning, undertake impact analyses, and are knowledgeable about a range of techniques to involve the public in planning. Public school officials engage in a variety of planning processes at the systemwide level as well as at the individual school level. Here, too, planners might assist by offering their services as process experts.

A number of city school districts are engaged in Year 2000, or comparably labeled, strategic planning programs. Planners should seek opportunities to get involved in such programs, offering their assistance in helping to design and facilitate them. They could also serve as resource people on some strategic issue subcommittees (e.g., financing, school-community relations, capital improvements). If some educational reforms are getting serious attention, planners might help by providing technical advice (e.g., for a controlled choice program, for example, planners could assist in providing demographic data to determine the racial and ethnic mix for different zones in the city). Planners might also assist in doing impact analyses to determine the effects of various reforms (e.g., a voucher plan, a metropolitan school desegregation plan, school-based management) on the community at large.

At the individual school level, there might also be opportunities for planners to play a helpful role. As the trend towards school-based management continues, which seems certain to happen, individual schools will need to plan more efficiently. They will need to assess their strengths and weaknesses, establish attainable goals, set priorities, and involve parents and community representatives in school governance. Planners, especially those working at the neighborhood level, could serve as process helpers to the school management teams in their planning efforts.

Regardless of the level at which planners try to get into the urban education system, their chances of doing so will increase if they can show urban educators that they are informed about issues, strategies, and reforms in the urban education arena. Knowledge in this sense affords planners more legitimacy to play a more active role in the urban education system.

REFERENCES

Blank, Rolf. 1989. "Educational Effects of Magnet Schools." Paper presented for Conference on Choice and Control in American Education, University of Wisconsin-Madison.

Brozan, Nadine. 1990. "From Citibank: Millions for Schools." *New York Times,* May 16, 1990.

The Carnegie Foundation for the Advancement of Teaching. 1988. An Imperiled Generation: Saving Urban Schools. Princeton, N.J.: The Carnegie Foundation for the Advancement of Teaching.

Celis, William. 1992. "Businesslike with Business's Help, Cincinnati Schools Shake Off Crisis." *New York Times,* August 20, 1992.

Chicago Panel on Public School Policy and Finance. 1987. *Dropouts From the Chicago Public Schools.*

Chira, Susan. 1992. "Research Questions Effectiveness of Most School-Choice Programs." *New York Times,* October 26, 1992.

_____. 1993. "Rethinking Deliberately Segregated Schools." *New York Times,* July 11, 1993.

_____. 1993. "Student Poll Finds Wide Use of Guns." *New York Times,* July 20, 1993.

Chubb, John and Moe, Terry. 1990. *Politics, Markets and America's Schools.* Washington, D.C.: The Brookings Institution.

Coleman, James. 1966. *Equality of Equal Opportunity.* Washington, D.C.: U.S. Government Printing Office.

Coons, John and Sugerman, Stephen. 1978. *Education by Choice: The Case for Family Control.* Berkeley: The University of California Press.

Council of Great City Schools. 1987. *Condition of Great City Schools: 1980-86.* Washington, D.C.: Council of Great City Schools.

Daniels, Lee. 1989. "The Winning Ways to Desegregate the Schools." *New York Times,* December 17, 1989.

Finn, Chester. 1991. *We Must Take Charge: Our Schools and Our Future*. New York: The Free Press.

Folbre, Nancy. 1992. "Business to the Rescue." *The Nation*, September 21, 1992.

Gardner, Howard. 1991. *The Unschooled Mind*. New York: Basic Books.

Greider, William. 1992. "Stand and Deliver." *Rolling Stone*, August 20, 1992.

Hill, Paul. 1992. "Urban Education." In *Urban America: Policy Choices for Los Angeles and the Nation*, edited by James Steinberg, David Lyon, and Mary Vaiana. Santa Monica: Rand.

Kolderie, Ted. 1992. "Chartering Diversity." *Equity and Choice* 9, no. 1.

Kozol, Jonathon. 1991. *Savage Inequalities: Children in America's Schools*. New York: Crown Publishers.

Lemann, Nicholas. 1991. "A False Panacea." *The Atlantic Monthly*, January 1991.

National Commission on Excellence in Education. 1983. *A Nation At Risk: The Imperative for Educational Reform*. Washington, D.C.: U. S. Government Printing Office.

New York City Planning Commission. 1993. *Shaping The City's Future*.

Orfield, Gary. 1988. *Segregated Housing, Educational Inequality and the Possibility of Urban Integration*. Washington, D.C.: The Urban Institute.

Ornstein, Allan. 1988. "State Financing of Public Schools." *Urban Education* 23, no. 2.

Payne, Charles. 1991. "The Comer Intervention Model and School Reform in Chicago: Implications of Two Models of Change." *Urban Education* 26, no. 1.

_____. 1987. *Getting What We Ask For: The Ambiguity of Success and Failure in Urban Education*. Greenwood Press.

Rankin, Robert. 1992. "Helping Residents Rebuild a Blighted Community." *The Philadelphia Inquirer*, May 24, 1992.

Robbins, William. 1990. "School Plan Stirs Kansas City Debate." *New York Times*, April 5, 1990.

Seattle Planning Department. 1993. *The Seattle Comprehensive Plan: Toward a Sustainable Seattle.*

Shanker, Albert. 1992. "Chelsea Three Years Later." *New York Times*, October 4, 1992.

Sizer, Theodore. 1984. *Horace's Compromise: The Dilemma of the American High School.* Boston: Houghton Mifflin Company.

Steinbach, Carol. 1988. "Investing Early." *National Journal*, September 3, 1988.

Verhovek, Sam. 1993. "Texas to Hold Referendum on School-Aid Shift to Poor." *New York Times*, February 16, 1993.

Walters, Laurel. 1991. "Buzzword for the 90's: Choice." *The Christian Science Monitor*, March 11, 1991.

vanderWeele, Marybeth. 1993. "Is Public Patience Wearing Thin?" *Chicago Sun-Times*, March 28, 1993.

Wells, Amy. 1990. "Milwaukee Parents Get More Choice on Schools." *New York Times*, 1990.

_____. 1990. "Preschool Program in New York City is Reported to Surpass Head Start." *New York Times*, May 16, 1990.

_____. 1989. "For Slow Learners, an Accelerated Curriculum." *New York Times*, May 31, 1989.

Wilkerson, Isabel. 1992. "Des Moines Acts to Halt White Flight After State Allows Choice of Schools." *New York Times*, December 16, 1992.

Witte, John. 1990. *Choice in American Education.* Madison: University of Wisconsin, Robert LaFollette Institute of Public Affairs.

Jerome L. Kaufman is a professor in the Department of Urban and Regional Planning at the University of Wisconsin in Madison. Kenneth C. Newman is a graduate student in that same department.

8

Planning, Community Policing, and Neighborhood Revitalization

By N. David Milder

INTRODUCTION[1]

Planning in the 1990s must become more comprehensive, with a broadened set of considerations defining the outlook and responsibilities of practitioners. This essay will detail why planners should become more professionally involved with safety and security issues and how they can demonstrate that their knowledge and skills are well-suited for formulating effective neighborhood solutions to these problems.

The Impacts of Crime on Urban Planning

Planners must consider the impacts of crime in order to create realistic plans. Taub, Taylor, and Dunham, for example, found that negative perceptions of neighborhood safety strongly reduce the likelihood that home owners will invest in the maintenance or enhancement of their properties (1984:136). They also found that "satisfaction with neighborhood safety is the strongest single predictor of intentions to move." (1984:177). The fear of crime can turn attractive neighborhood parks into liabilities that reinforce the desire of local residents to move

(Skogan 1989:22). Fear can also keep people from using subways and buses (MTA 1988:24).

Crime is a very important consideration in business locational decisions. For example, a national survey of firms in the health care industry found that crime was the most important criterion they use to select sites for office, laboratory, manufacturing, or distribution facilities (Milder 1992:36). In an earlier survey, major corporations headquartered in Manhattan ranked crime third among 19 criteria they used to evaluate potential back office sites (Armstrong and Milder 1985:15).

The City of New York has spent millions of dollars over the past four years to provide 3,000 "formerly homeless and often drug-troubled families" with rehabbed housing located in South Bronx neighborhoods well known for their problems with drugs, prostitution, and street violence. Moreover, few of the social services required to support such needy and vulnerable families were being provided for on or near these buildings. Consequently, much of this housing is now in trouble. In one building rehabbed for 43 families at the cost of $3 million, "the front door is left open to drug dealers, the elevator doesn't work, several apartments are padlocked as a result of fires and the halls are covered with graffiti," according to *Newsday*. Once again the "good guys" appear to have lost to the "bad guys," giving neighborhood residents cause for despair.

These are grim stories for planners to ponder. However, there is a new variable that could begin to alter the equation in communities across the country. Police departments are adopting a community policing patrol strategy. While most media attention has focused on the use of foot patrol officers, the real key to this strategy's success is the mobilization of segments of the neighborhood, such as residents, businessmen, churches, and hospitals, to join the police in solving local concerns about crime and disorder (see for example NIJ 1992b and McElroy *et al* 1993:10).

In these efforts, the police can display a surprisingly "broad vision," with neighborhood security and quality of life issues inseparably linked: A safe and secure neighborhood needs not only cops on patrol, but also buildings in good repair, clean streets, adults with jobs, safe and effective schools with ample recreation facilities for children. Every time a police department adopts a community policing strategy, it implicitly issues an invitation to planners, asking them to contribute their skills to the municipality's crime prevention and fear reduction efforts.

Police are not alone in this effort. Today, in many cities, a variety of neighborhood-level organizations are the real engines of economic and community development. They may be known as Community Development Corporations (CDCs) or Local Development Corporations (LDCs). Central business districts also may have organizations of their own which may or may not be LDCs or be associated with a special downtown district management organization. For purposes of brevity and clarity, all of these organizations shall be referred to as local development organizations, or LDOs.[2] These LDOs employ a large number of people who are engaged in planning activities.

Most LDOs now have the same knowledge and awareness of crime and community policing as the rest of the planning profession. But, prior to community policing's popularity, a few LDOs were motivated by their local security needs to identify and develop staff planning capabilities and programs that will allow them to play functionally important roles under a community policing strategy.

Their work needs to be properly disseminated and expanded upon. Local planning departments can be of considerable help in this regard and doing so promises significant benefits, especially for crime-plagued, "underclass" neighborhoods.

An informed planning profession, with its training and networking assets, can be of great value to the LDOs as they rise to meet this challenge. APA's participation in inter-professional conferences with such organizations as the American Institute of Architects, the Association of Collegiate Schools of Architecture, and the U.S. Conference of Mayors on how physical design conditions can impact crime and the fear of crime can also be of considerable benefit.

WHAT IS COMMUNITY POLICING?

After World War II, police departments adopted the "crime attack" model of crime prevention and law enforcement. Officers were taken off neighborhood foot patrols and placed into cars so they could cover larger areas and respond more quickly to crime scenes. But research has since shown that preventive car patrols and rapid response to calls have little impact on crime, fears, or a community's satisfaction with the police. Unfortunately, this reactive strategy made the police aloof from citizens and their neighborhoods.

Today, departments are adopting policing strategies that emphasize close cooperation between police officers and local citizens in active efforts to solve local crime problems, improve the quality of life, and create defensible neighborhoods.

While community or problem-oriented policing programs will take different forms in different communities, they will all be predicated on police officers working closely with local citizens to *identify and solve the neighborhood's problems associated with preventing crime and reducing the fear of victimization* (McElroy et al 1993). Whether the police utilize more foot patrols or have other patrol officers increase their contacts with local residents, community policing will place great emphasis on identifying and remediating the underlying conditions that foster criminal activities and citizen fears. This emphasis on problem solving means that practitioners of community policing are often interested in non-patrol[3] solutions that make it difficult and less rewarding for criminals to operate in a particular area.

For community policing to work, the local police must have effective and empowered neighborhood partners. The strategy needs local leaders and neighborhood organizations who can really get things done, who can take the "initiative in preventing and solving crimes" (NIJ 1992A:4).

This implies that this policing strategy might have the least potential for success in neighborhoods where the police are most obviously needed, those with the highest crime rates and levels of social disorder. Such neighborhoods tend to be poor and disadvantaged, with weak family units and few effective social organizations, such as churches, recreational groups, or neighborhood organizations. As Wilson has noted:

> . . . the communities of the underclass are plagued by massive joblessness, flagrant and open lawlessness and low-achieving schools, and therefore tend to be avoided by outsiders. Consequently, the residents of these areas, whether women and children of welfare families or aggressive street criminals have

increasingly been socially isolated from mainstream patterns of behavior. (Wilson, 1987:58)

In these defenseless neighborhoods, the police are left to play—as much as their resources will allow—a primarily "protective" role. Police resources might be insufficient to cope with the massive problems of prostitution, street violence, and burglaries associated with the drug use and possession of sophisticated weapons that often typify these neighborhoods. Faced with this crime syndrome, it is not unusual for local residents and businessmen to demand what amounts to a perpetual police crackdown.

Community policing tries to use roles and activities that are more traditionally associated with providing social services and community and economic development. A defensible neighborhood, after all, is one in which residents can expect to enjoy an acceptable quality of life. A physically and socially deteriorated neighborhood is much more porous to crime. In one deteriorated housing complex, for example, cracks around the doors and windows made it easy for burglars to break in. Vacant units, too badly deteriorated to rent, were used by burglars and drug addicts (Spelman and Eck, 1987-5).

Officers imbued with community policing values can be expected to try mobilize other public agencies or even to organize and empower neighborhood residents (McElroy et al 1993:9-10). But this means that these officers will be pulled toward playing roles that are far beyond their training and job descriptions and that take large amounts of time away from their more "normal" duties. For example:

- In Newport News, Virginia, police became concerned about a 450-unit housing complex which was badly deteriorated and had the highest crime rate in the city. They first worked with other city departments (e.g., fire, sanitation, public works, code compliance) to have the complex fixed up and the area cleaned up. Later the police proposed a plan for closing the complex and moving tenants to better housing. This involved developing plans for a new 220-unit housing complex with a middle school and a small shopping center (Spelman and Eck, 1987:5-6).

- In Oakland, California, officers assigned to the downtown district worked with nearby schools and truant officers to reduce the numbers of teenagers hanging out and often getting into trouble in the area (Reiss, 1985).

- In New York City, a Community Patrol Officer Program (CPOP) "effectively organized area residents to clean their blocks" and worked closely with the community board to get abandoned buildings sealed so that they could not be used by drug dealers (McElroy et al 1993:200-201).

It is likely that in neighborhoods unable to defend themselves, more will be asked of police than they can reasonably be expected to accomplish.

Consequently, caretaker-partners in poor, high-crime neighborhoods can be of great value to the police and greatly increase the effectiveness of existing police resources. Successful LDOs have the organizational and community development skills and operational relationships with such municipal departments as housing, economic development, fire, sanitation, traffic enforcement, and public works to be able to play such a role.

Even weak neighborhoods may not be entirely bereft of the social and organizational resources needed to defend themselves. Many of them have a hospital, various types of businesses, or a college. Often the businesses are organized into local development corporations, chambers of commerce, or even special assessment districts. Residents may have formed neighborhood organizations, though these often lack sufficient financial and political resources. In some instances, effective community organizations from other neighborhoods might be brought in by local officials. This happened in the Hunts Point neighborhood in the Bronx, where new housing units are being developed and managed by community groups that demonstrated their effectiveness in other Bronx neighborhoods.

In these weak urban neighborhoods, organizational resources are typically fragmented and isolated. Businessmen typically will have little or nothing to do with local residents or the nearby hospital or college. Residents may view local businessmen as "foreigners," if not enemies. Such neighborhood fracturing is often reinforced by social and racial differences, such as when the businessmen are white or Asian, and the residents are black or Hispanic.

This fragmentation was encouraged by the roles and expectations assigned to the public under the old crime attack model. The public's role under this model was generally confined to reporting crimes, providing information, and taking proper security precautions with their own persons and property. Residents were encouraged to "harden" their homes against burglaries by installing the proper doors, windows, locks, and alarms. Perhaps they were asked to participate in passive neighborhood watches, where they would use telephone trees to report suspicious persons or crimes to their neighbors and the police. Businessmen were encouraged to employ comparable site hardening and crime watch programs. But the businessmen were not linked with the residents to combat the problems of disorder that often plagued both groups.

By adopting a fortress-type security posture, businesses withdrew from the local neighborhood. As Kelling and Stewart have noted about such behavior:

> A person who withdraws behind heavy doors and substantial locks, armed with a guard dog and weapons, and who refuses to interact with neighbors, even to the extent of observing behavior in the street, may be detracting from the self-defense of the community rather than contributing to it. Such behavior may well be an example of poor citizenship and irresponsibility rather than prudent civil behavior. (Kelling and Stewart, 1989:4).

This penchant for a fortress security posture meant businesses could have no "caretaker" role in the surrounding area nor take any responsibility for creating a defensible neighborhood. Most firms kept away from nearby residential areas, schools, or shelters—although most of those burglarizing their buildings, mugging their employees and customers, or engaging in disorderly behavior came from these places. Neighborhood organizations were discouraged by most police departments from taking any active steps to make their residential area more secure.

A 1988 study sponsored by the National Institute of Justice found that while it was not rare for businessmen and residents to interact on neighborhood crime prevention programs, it was far from usual (Milder, 1988:2). In most instances, these efforts were initiated by residential organizations to help protect and retain local merchants. Occasionally, a very large firm, such as Pfizer, might initiate a neighborhood security program, although hospitals and universities were more likely to do so. These neighborhood caretakers tended to take the roles of protectors, parents, partners, and cornerstones,[4] roles that LDOs might usefully perform under a community policing strategy.

Here is how the four roles are defined:

Protectors. Neighborhood organizations will sometimes create a crime prevention program to *protect* a group they want to keep in the neighborhood. For example:

- In Chicago, the Back-of-the-Yards neighborhood residential organization canvasses local merchants about security problems and then puts pressure on local police to deal with these problems.

- Also in Chicago, the Northeast Austin organization patrols the perimeter of a local hospital.

- In Erie, Pennsylvania, after meeting with local residents, the security staff of the St. Vincent Health Center implemented a patrol covering homes within a six-block radius of the hospital.

- In Brooklyn, N.Y., Pfizer has installed closed circuit TV cameras and "talk-back" boxes in the Flushing Avenue subway station. Its security force also patrols the area outside the station. While many Pfizer employees use the station, the vast majority of the 396,000 passengers entering annually are local residents. Pfizer's security patrol also regularly covers a nearby school for the emotionally disturbed.

Parents. One of the most difficult things that an organization can do is parent a new organization for an entirely different membership group: for example, a residential organization organizes local retailers into a merchants association. It usually demands that the parent devote a full-time staff person to the project. Such a project is a good measure of the importance the benefiting group has for the parent. Some examples of neighborhood organizations playing a parent role are:

- In Brooklyn, N.Y., the Flatbush Development Corporation, an essentially homeowner/residential organizations has organized and manages three local merchant associations.

- In Portland, Oregon, a neighborhood association helped retailers on commercial strips on Hawthorne, Belmont, and Division streets to form their own retail associations.

- Pfizer has helped local merchants organize and form their own security program.

- An areawide security plan recently submitted to the Hunts Point LDC recommends that it work with other nonprofits to immediately get a community organizer into the area to help apartment buildings not yet taken over by drug dealers and homeowners to organize.

Partners. In partnership programs, members from two or more segments of the neighborhood work actively together on a crime prevention program. For example:

- In the Euclid-Maryland neighborhood of St. Louis, local property owners, merchants, residents, precinct police officers, and aldermen participate in an ad hoc committee to deal with nuisance crimes such as loitering, disturbing the peace, and traffic congestion during the warmer months between Easter and Labor Day. The crimes were badly affecting businesses and residents were being harassed.

- In Minneapolis, the Whitier Alliance (a CDC in which businessmen, residents and representatives from nearby museums and colleges play strong roles) has formed a partnership with local police to fight prostitution and associated street robberies on the main retail strip. Key has been the development of a close working relationship between the alliance's security director and the local vice squad, with which she meets three or four times a week.

As a result the police make regular sweeps of the strip and reveal names of arrested "johns." The police and the alliance have a shared strategy, with each partner doing what is appropriate for it. The police concentrate on the supply side of the prostitution problem, while the alliance tries to reduce demand.

Development Cornerstones. In or near many decayed urban areas are large businesses, hospitals, or colleges for which a move would mean costs in the hundreds of millions of dollars. For many of these organizations it is more cost effective to try to revitalize the neighborhoods than to move. With their financial resources, organizational skills, and political clout, these organizations quickly become "cornerstones"—the prime caretakers and key cogs in the redevelopment of their neighborhoods. They become involved in a wide range of issues, including housing, transportation, and retail development. Pfizer in Brooklyn, the University of Chicago, and the Ralston Purina Company in St. Louis are some examples of these cornerstones.

Pfizer's track record illustrates what a development cornerstone does and how it almost naturally gets into dealing with neighborhood crime problems. To redevelop the area around its Brooklyn plant, Pfizer put forward a $120 million project involving 200 housing units and more industrial space. But the plant's management realized this investment would not be secure unless the company improved ties among neighborhood groups and organizations and tried to improve their viability.

So Pfizer became active on the board of the local hospital and worked to get a community leader from the Marcy housing projects on the board. It established personal working relationships with merchants, a black cultural center, and a Hasidic group. It furnished office space to the Marcy Houses Tenant Association and provided a local church with technical assistance for its housing rehabilitation program.

Pfizer also became the cornerstone of the neighborhood's crime prevention efforts, performing at various times the protector, parent, and partner roles. Pfizer carries out security audits for other neighborhood organizations and tried to facilitate the creation of a security patrol and a Youth Elderly Escort Program by tenants in the Marcy Houses.

Pfizer communicates regularly with precinct commanders and uses its access to the mayor's office and the police commissioner to make sure the neighborhood is getting its share of attention from the department. Pfizer's attorneys follow up any arrest made in the area with the police and the district attorney's office. The attorneys are specifically instructed to go after drug dealers.

Some LDOs have succeeded in becoming development cornerstones. The Whitier Alliance plays such a role in its neighborhood, as does such New York City entities as the Greater Jamaica Development Corporation, SOBRO, and SEBCO. But LDOs have not been as successful in becoming neighborhood crime prevention cornerstones. Few have security forces or multimillion dollar capital investments to protect.

Planners Can Help Create Anti-Crime Cornerstones

LDOs have an enormous potential for serving as the cornerstones of defensible communities because of their broad economic and community development missions, memberships, contacts with government agencies, organizational and planning capabilities, fund-raising talents, and demonstrated abilities to generally get things done.

Planning departments can help LDOs in their community make the transition through workshops and seminars as well as by creating LDO networks where groups can discuss their roles under community policing, review common problems, and exchange success stories.

Planning departments can also help LDOs by supplying vital data and analysis services, such as a geographic information system that enables the LDOs to bring census data, real property and land use information, crime statistics, traffic and pedestrian counts into any security analysis. Organizations such as the American Planning Association can help planners learn that their normal day-to-day work on a project's location, its design, and the type of tenants envisioned for it can have fateful impacts on crime and fear levels in the project's vicinity. Project and urban designs consequently must become more security conscious.

It is important that LDOs—and the planners that work for them or with them—recognize some basic facts:

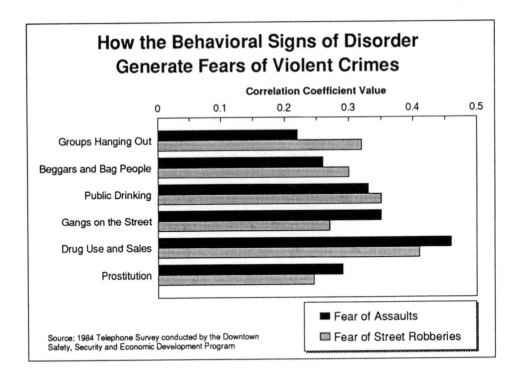

How the Behavioral Signs of Disorder Generate Fears of Violent Crimes

Correlation Coefficient Value

Groups Hanging Out

Beggars and Bag People

Public Drinking

Gangs on the Street

Drug Use and Sales

Prostitution

■ Fear of Assaults

▦ Fear of Street Robberies

Source: 1984 Telephone Survey conducted by the Downtown Safety, Security and Economic Development Program

Dealing with the signs of disorder should be a high priority for LDOs. These signs indicate that "no one is in charge of this place" and will be interpreted by the average citizen as good reasons to become afraid (Kelling and Wilson 1982, Skogan 1989). Some behavioral signs of disorder are the public use or sale of drugs and alcohol; teenagers clogging sidewalks; disoriented people who are drugged, drunk, or mentally unstable; and prostitution. Physical signs of disorder include broken windows, vacant buildings, graffiti, dirty streets and sidewalks, broken street lights, and broken park benches.

For businesses, crime and public disorder in local residential areas will make it much harder for them to stay in business, much less to expand. These areas probably house the neighborhood's major perpetrators, but also serve as the prime labor shed for local firms and the core area of customers for neighborhood retailers.

Residents must recognize that crime and disorder in the local business district affects their quality of life by diminishing the availability of goods and services in the neighborhood. Also, such areas can become operational bases for drug dealers, addicts, and prostitutes.

The police will never have sufficient resources to cope with a city's crime problems. According to the Office of Management Analysis and Planning of the NYPD, the number of felony arrests in New York City increased from 14,174 in 1950 to 157,160 in 1990. If the department's uniformed manpower had increased proportionately, it would have had 210,697 uniformed officers instead of 26,882.

The defensibility of a neighborhood against crime depends on the strength of all segments of the neighborhood and the level of cooperation among them.

Very few LDOs do an adequate job of analyzing their crime problems. Few obtain data from the police and map them out so they can learn the hot spots for various crimes. Few regularly survey their members to learn what the chief complaints are, and fewer analyze such data to understand how crime is really hurting local residents or businesses. As a consequence, many LDOs are dealing with the symptoms of problems rather than their causes. LDOs need to work closely with the police. This is essential if they are to truly adopt the problem-solving approach that is a major component of community policing. A thorough analysis can also help consensus-building by clarifying the importance of various security problems and identifying their causes.

Planners should remember that security considerations ought to be important factors in the siting and design of neighborhood residences, commercial structures, and public facilities. Here are some illustrative considerations, selected for their diversity:

- A residential building's height and design can affect crime rates by impacting on the probability that a potential perpetrator will be observed in common areas (Newman and Frank 1982).

- Designs exist for high security shopping centers for such neighborhoods as South Central Los Angeles that are able to withstand even riots and still provide vital retail services that rival those available in suburban shopping centers (Titus 1990, 1992).

- Security designs should provide clear lines of sight, good lighting, and few hiding places in public garages and subway stations.

- Generating ample pedestrian traffic in commercial areas can reduce fear. This means having a degree of dense, compact, multifunctional development that is commensurate with the amount of space to be provided by a project (Milder 1985).

- Do not place facilities that will attract large groups of teenagers, such as an after-school bus transfer point, next to a major retail center. Large numbers of even the most innocent, normally behaved teenagers can induce fears among elderly and female shoppers (Milder 1987).

Private neighborhood patrols are often the first thing that LDOs consider, but they may not be the most effective or efficient way to deal with a problem. For instance:

- Crowds of youths congregating in downtown commercial areas might be effectively dispersed by having schools stagger their release times, or restricting school bus passes to fewer afternoon hours, as was done in Cleveland (Milder et al 1985).

- In downtown Tulsa, the development organization sponsors a program that recruits homeless alcoholics and drug users into a detoxification program that has an employment component (Milder et al 1985).

- Traffic barriers are being used to keep drug users away from drug dealers in Lawrence, Massachusetts; Bridgeport, Connecticut; Miami; and Portland, Oregon. Traffic barriers have also been successfully used in London to curb prostitution (Mathews 1990).

- Mothers in Metheun, Massachusetts, are fighting prostitution by using videotapes to scare away men seeking prostitutes (*NY Times* 3/21/93).

- Providing an off-street parking lot where autos could congregate substantially reduced a "cruising" problem in Arlington, Texas (Bell and Burk 1989).

- A new health care center in Jamaica Center, New York, will be made graffiti-resistant by a glazed-block exterior from which graffiti can be removed quickly and easily (*NY Times* 7/11/93).

A defensible community has caretakers. When they work together under a formal strategy, they will be even more effective and the community will be even stronger. LDOs, along with the local police precinct command, should create a Neighborhood Enhancement Committee in which the strongest organizations active in the neighborhood are invited to participate. These can be large private sector firms, such as Pfizer, neighborhood residential groups, block associations, businesses and business associations, major churches, large hospitals, universities, colleges, museums, and other cultural and arts organizations.

Today, in the best of circumstances, there will be communication and information-sharing between precinct police officers and LDOs and local businessmen. But if community policing is to work properly, cooperation and communication between the local police, local residents, and the business community must shift to an even higher level. LDOs might help the police be more effective in their neighborhoods by:

- Being the contact with city agencies to lobby for actions the local police have identified as needed; e.g., getting the city to board up buildings being used by drug dealers or prostitutes, getting the schools to alter their release times, and getting the lighting on key streets made substantially brighter.

- Having the LDO security personnel work in a coordinated manner with the police on specific problems as does the Whitier Alliance in Minneapolis and the Grand Central Partnership in Manhattan.

- Publicly showing appreciation, especially to individual officers, when the police do a good job.

CONCLUSIONS

Under a community policing strategy, both LDOs and the police see a healthy community in the same way: it is empowered, has public order, and enjoys a good quality of life. The police need strong and effective neighborhood organizations as partners if this strategy is to succeed. But LDOs must take on new responsibilities for public safety and the maintenance of order in their neighborhoods, because public safety and order require a real community. LDOs have the economic and community development skills, organizational capability, neighborhood and government contacts, and ability to innovate that the police can never hope to duplicate without jeopardizing their own mission.

Planners As Coordinators

Behind all this will be the ever-present need for planners capable of bringing together residents, local businesses, local institutions, and the police to forge and implement a comprehensive areawide plan to make their neighborhoods defensible. The ability to analyze underlying causes and trends should also enable planners to be particularly adept at assuring that a project's location, design, and tenancy will help make the neighborhood safe and defensible. These same skills should also enable planners to formulate non-patrol solutions to neighborhood security problems, especially those associated with the signs of disorder.

The establishment of a Neighborhood Enhancement Committee charged with improving the local quality of life promises to be an effective way to both initiate and formalize the new partnership between the police, the LDO, and other important community actors. One of the first tasks this committee can tackle is the formulation of a joint areawide security strategy that establishes a local consensus on security priorities and assigns each participant organization clear roles and responsibilities, while outlining how their activities can be coordinated.

If such partnerships between the police, LDOs, and planners can be forged, then we may truly see a significant reduction in our urban crime problems.

NOTES

1. The author would like to thank Capt. Pasquale Petrino, William B. Shore, Frank So, Jr., Richard Titus, and Adam Zalma for their comments on one or more drafts of this article.

2. In smaller municipalities the planning department and/or other municipal agencies may be carrying out the functions of an LDO.

3. Non-patrol activities are those that do not involve the use of police or private security personnel on beat patrols or in the pursuit and apprehension of criminals, though they may be used in conjunction with them. Community policing is thus very similar to situational crime prevention and CPTED (Crime Prevention Through Environmental Design) approaches (Clarke 1992:5-7).

4. The following discussion of protectors, parents, partners, and cornerstones is all based on Milder, 1988.

SELECT BIBLIOGRAPHY

Armstrong, Regina B., and N. David Milder. 1985. "Employment in the Manhattan CBD and Back Office Locational Decisions," *City Almanac*, Vol. 18, Nos. 1-2.

Bell, John, and Barbara Burke. 1989. "Cruising Cooper Street," *Police Chief*, January: 26-29.

Clark, Ronald V. 1992. *Situational Crime Prevention: Successful Case Studies.* Albany, N.Y.: Harrow and Heston.

Guyot, Dorothy 1991. *Policing As Though People Matter.* Philadelphia: Temple University Press.

Kelling, George L. 1988. "Police and Communities: the Quiet Revolution," *Perspectives on Policing*, No. 1, The National Institute of Justice, Washington, D.C.

_____ and Maryalice Sloan-Howitt. 1990. "Subway Graffiti in New York City: 'Gettin Up' vs. 'Meanin It and Cleanin It,'" *Security Journal*, 1: 131-136.

_____ and James K. Stewart 1989. "Neighborhoods and Police: The Maintenance of Civil Authority, *Perspectives on Policing*, No. 10, The National Institute of Justice, Washington, D.C.

_____ and James Q. Wilson. 1982. "The Police and Neighborhood Safety," *The Atlantic Monthly*, March 1982, pp. 492-504.

Mathews, Roger. 1990. "Developing More Effective Strategies for Curbing Prostitution," *Security Journal* 1: 182-187.

McElroy, James E., Colleen A. Musgrove and Susan Sadd. 1993. *Community Policing: The CPOP in New York*. Newbury Park, N.Y.: Sage Publications.

Metropolitan Transportation Authority. 1988. *Crime and Personal Security in the Subway: New Yorkers' Perceptions*. New York: MTA.

Milder, N. David, et al 1985. *Downtown Safety, Security and Economic Development*. New York: Downtown Research and Development Center.

Milder, N. David. 1987. "Crime and Downtown Revitalization," *Urban Land*, September 1987, pp. 16-19.

_____ 1988. *Protectors, Parents, Partners and Cornerstones: Types of Neighborhood Cooperative Crime Prevention Programs*. Kew Gardens, N.Y.: DANTH Associates.

_____ 1990. *An Areawide Security Program for the Hunts Point Industrial Park*, Kew Gardens, N.Y.: DANTH Associates.

_____1992. *The Gun Hill Atrium: A Project Feasibility Study*. Kew Gardens, N.Y.: DANTH Associates.

NIJ. 1992. "Community Policing in the 1990's," *National Institute of Justice Journal*, August 1992, pp. 2-8.

_____ 1992. "Community Policing in Seattle: A Model Partnership Between Citizens and Police," *National Institute of Justice Journal*, August 1992, pp. 9-15.

Newman, Oscar, and Karen A. Frank. 1982. "The Effects of Building Size on Personal Crime and Fear of Crime," *Population and Environment*, Vol. 5, No. 4 Winter 1982. pp. 203-220.

Pate, Anthony Michael. 1989. "Community-Oriented Policing in Baltimore" in Dennis Jay Kenney ed). *Police and Policing: Contemporary Issues*, pp. 112-135, New York: Prager.

Poyner, Barry, and Barry Webb. 1987. "Reducing Theft from Shopping Bags in City Center Markets," in Poyner and Webb eds.. *Successful Crime Prevention: Case Studies*. London: Tranistock Institute.

Poyner, Barry. 1991. "Situational Crime Prevention in Two Parking Facilities," *Security Journal* 2:96-101.

Reis, Albert J. 1985. *Policing a City's Central District: The Oakland Story*. Washington, D.C.: The National Institute of Justice.

Skogan, Wesley G. 1989. *Disorder and Decline: Crime and the Spiral of Decay in American Neighborhoods*. New York: Free Press.

Spelman, William, and John Eck. 1987. "Newport News Tests Problem-Oriented Policing," *NIJ Reports*, January-February, 1987.

Taub, Richard P., D. Garth Taylor and Jan D. Dunham. 1984. *Paths of Neighborhood Change: Race and Crime in America*. Chicago: University of Chicago Press.

Titus, Richard. 1990. "Security Works: Shopping Enclaves Bring Hope, Investment to Blighted Inner-City Neighborhoods," *Urban Land*, January 1990, pp. 2-5.

_____ 1992. "Development Opportunities in the Inner City," *NIJ*, Washington, D.C., June 1992, pp. 1-8.

Trojanowicz, Robert, et al. 1984. *An Evaluation of the Neighborhood Foot Patrol in Flint, Michigan*. Flint, Mich.: Michigan State University.

Wilson, William Julius. 1987. *The Truly Disadvantaged: The Inner City, the Underclass and Public Policy*. Chicago: University of Chicago Press.

N. David Milder is a principal of DANTH associates, an economic development consulting firm based in Kew Gardens, New York. Long aware that crime and the fear of crime can impede urban economic development, he has developed security plans for downtown Brooklyn, Jamaica Center, and the Hunts Point Industrial Park. His approach to these plans was formed during a number of research projects, such as the Downtown Safety, Security and Economic Development Program he directed for the Regional Plan Association.

9

Citizen Participation: Whose Vision Is It?

By William R. Klein, AICP

I know of no safe depository of the ultimate powers of this society but the people themselves; and if we think them not enlightened enough to exercise their control with a wholesome discretion, the remedy is not to take it from them, but to inform their discretion.
Thomas Jefferson
Letter to William Charles Jarvis, September 28, 1820

Planners often find themselves in the role of broker, resolving conflicts and disputes in the interest of the long-range future of our nation's communities. Decision makers must be in touch with good information concerning characteristics and trends of the community, but they must also be in touch with the aspirations, values, and visions of the citizens they serve. The two-way street Jefferson alluded to—of citizen influence on the public decision-making process and leaders' influence through informing the citizenry—continues to be familiar territory for planners who are doing their job well.

The problem comes when planners and public officials try to serve the interests of the minority in the face of a citizen participation process that may be heavily weighted to protect the interests of the majority. That is the subject of this paper. It is our purpose here not to provide

answers but to frame the questions that will lead to appropriate answers to this dilemma. Addressed to the community planning professional, this paper will identify citizen participation issues for the 1990s
and beyond, particularly those involving equity. It will summarize
some of the innovative forms of structured involvement that have
emerged in the past five years, drawing upon examples that show
promise for protecting the interests of low-income and minority neighborhoods and other traditionally underrepresented populations. The
paper closes with eight summary points.

FAMILIAR TERRITORY

The design and execution of effective programs to involve citizenry at
all stages of the community development process have been subjects of
interest to planners for some time. In the last several years especially,
there has been a dramatic upsurge in citizen involvement activity across
the country. Small towns, large cities, and even metropolitan regions
are beginning to appreciate, as never before, the notion that plans have
a greater chance of being implemented when citizens play a meaningful
role in shaping them. Stakeholders must feel ownership of the plan.
Divergent interests must be brought to the table to identify common
values. Planning should be a bottom-up process involving the very
people that plans affect most—citizens. Effective and equitable community participation, however, can be an elusive and troublesome thing to
achieve.

Despite renewed interest in citizen participation generally, there is
serious doubt as to whether the benefits of such involvement extend to
the interests of some of the nation's most distressed communities and
neighborhoods. Minority and lower-income sections of older inner cities
are often functionally isolated from such processes. Differences in
language, race, ethnicity, culture, educational attainment, and experience with government process can become impediments to citizen
involvement in the planning and urban revitalization process —a
process that more often than not is conducted downtown.

There is another side to citizen participation that can run counter to the
interests of low-income and minority neighborhoods. When jurisdictions outside central cities blindly cater to citizen desires while exclud-
ing consideration of broader societal values and authority, the other
edge of the visioning sword presents itself. For instance, in Mount
Laurel, New Jersey, in Yonkers, New York, and most recently, in

Chester, Connecticut, community leaders were presumably in touch with the underlying community value structure when they enacted exclusionary zoning practices.

OLD-STYLE PARTICIPATION: THE TROUBLE WITH HEARINGS

Structured citizen participation is certainly not a new idea. Required public hearings, for instance, have been institutionalized within enabling statutes and regulations governing land use, environmental protection, and urban revitalization for many decades. In most states, hearings must be held for plan adoption, zoning changes, variances, special use permits, PUDs and PRDs, rights-of-way takings, condemnation, community development block grants, and most redevelopment activities.

Most federal programs require evidence of an open, participatory process. In 1978, the Federal Regional Council published *Citizen Participation*, a 140-page guide to the requirements of all federally assisted programs. While its glossary described 39 innovative techniques for engaging the public, most jurisdictions have kept their public participation process short and simple. That means meeting the minimum requirements, usually a public hearing.

The unfortunate thing is that the old-style processes all too often result in perfunctory, stilted, and "go through the motions" styles of engagement. With a few notable exceptions, these practices often pay only lip service to meaningful participation by the public and do so within a structure that is almost always organized from the top down. If citizens come at all, they often leave the hearing hall feeling ineffectual, co-opted, or manipulated. They leave believing that "the fix is in."

When comprehensive plans are prepared in the old style, a typical scenario calls for a draft plan to be drawn up by a consultant, or by planning commission staff, with only incidental, or ritualistic, input from working committees of citizens during the process. A citizen attitude survey is done. A final public hearing is held by the planning commission or city council at the end of the process. Sometimes, cosmetic changes are made to the draft, reflecting comments made at the hearing. However, the basic foundation of the plan, its value structure, and its assessment of problems and opportunities are set early in the program; they remain intact, for the most part unaffected by the public hearing process.

Public participation of this kind all too often involves experts explaining and seeking support for a completed plan. Planning is done *to* or *for* the public, not *with* the public. Citizen participation is pursued more to grease the skids for ultimate public acceptance of the project than to inform the substance of the plan. When public outcry causes plans or proposals to fail, it is always because the public has not understood the analysis of the experts—the public education efforts of the program have failed. Community leaders are to provide all the answers; the public is rarely mobilized or challenged to help solve tough problems.

Old-style public hearings, especially, fail as a medium for citizen participation. This is true for several reasons:

- Public hearings are often discounted by public officials due to their tendency to draw individuals who do not always fairly represent the interests of the community at large, or of neighborhoods, or of the long-range interests of the town, city, or region. The perception is that people who attend public hearings tend to feel strongly about the issues, often have extreme positions, and are there for a narrow purpose related to their own self-interest.

- Public hearings do not often represent a welcoming forum to individuals who may have strong and legitimate feelings but who do not have the knowledge, confidence, or verbal skills to talk in front of a group.

- Public hearings can be difficult to attend by reason of location, time of day, child care conflicts, or employment.

- Public hearings are often scheduled at the end of a process to respond to draft documents or plans that have already been drawn up. They rarely occur at the front end of the process where input can better shape the direction and value structure of the project.

- When meetings are "stacked" with proponents or opponents of a certain issue, decision makers may lose sight of the long-term interests of the community at large. It can be an environment in which NIMBYs (not in my back yard), LULUs (locally undesirable land uses), and NIMTOOs (not in my term of office) thrive.

The trouble with public hearings is that they are often too little and too late in the process.

A NEW ANGLE

We have begun to see the style and structure of citizen participation efforts in the past five years shift away from a sole reliance on the public hearing to new techniques. The new emerging systems are less paternalistic and condescending in their styles. They involve the various constituencies of the jurisdiction both in the initial visioning/goal-setting process, and the decision-making process when a plan is actually adopted. These participation systems often tacitly admit up front that planners or public officials do not have all the answers, that tough choices have to be made, and that resources are limited. They provide an atmosphere in which leaders can mobilize individuals and groups to help them solve hard problems.

The new techniques show promise for adaptation. Their flexibility can provide greater opportunities for participation by residents and business owners in our nations distressed urban areas.

A brief description of several of the more prevalent trends follows.

Visioning. In recent years, the U.S. has seen a marked resurgence and retooling of citizen involvement in planning—much of it involving a process that has come to be called "visioning." Small towns, large cities, and even metropolitan regions, have added elaborate public involvement processes to the front end of their comprehensive or strategic planning efforts. Drawing upon a wide variety of techniques, participants representing a broad spectrum of interests are brought together to reach agreement about a common vision of the future. Above all else, visioning is a value-laden process. Participants express what they like about their region, community, or neighborhood and want to protect; they also talk about what they don't like about their area and what they want to get rid of or improve. Proponents of visioning believe that when plans resonate well with the deeper aspirations and values of citizens, they have a greater chance of being implemented.

A look at recent visioning projects reveals that there has been a quantum shift in time and energy devoted to involvement and that the array of techniques has broadened significantly. While approaches vary widely, successful visioning processes share a number of common characteristics.

- Front-end emphasis. Visioning takes place well before the preparation of a plan.

- One size does not fit all. The process is tailored to the specific political, social, and physical terrain of the neighborhood, town, city, or region.

- It's inclusive. The process tries hard to involve people who rarely attend meetings—low-income and minority populations, business people, children, people with English as a second language, the elderly, renters, owners of large tracts of land, farmers, design professionals, developers, and bankers.

- Leadership is impartial. Professional facilitators, mediators, consultants, or nonprofit organizations are often called upon to help shape and guide the process.

- Attention to detail. Great care is taken in deciding about what use to be the most trivial matters: Where the meetings are held, how the chairs are arranged, who welcomes the participants, what equipment to use, and so on.

A Citizen Participation Sampler

Vision 2020, *Growth and Transportation Strategy for the Central Puget Sound Region*, Puget Sound Council of Governments, Washington

Fifty-seven local and county governments reached agreement on a long-range growth and transportation strategy for the central Puget Sound area. The council's efforts to involve and inform the public included symposiums, workshops, newspaper tabloid inserts, public hearings, open houses, surveys, and community meetings—the most extensive regional public involvement effort ever conducted in the area. The resulting publication is one of the clearest, most attractively designed statements of its kind. A resolution adopting the strategy was passed by the COG in October of 1990.

- Risks are taken. Community leadership gives up some of its authority, at least temporarily, in favor of a steering committee, a set of task forces, or some other group outside the traditional power structure.

- Projections are made. The process often uses various technical tools to help the community understand the consequences of alternative courses of action, such as computerized buildout projections, visual preference testing, and GIS.

- Media attention. Newspaper, cable and broadcast TV, and radio are central, not just important, participants in the process.

- Long-range thinking. Participants are urged to think about "this place" in 20 or 40 years, as opposed to the shorter horizons usually cited in more conventional processes.

- Results are validated. A document summarizing the vision is voted on or otherwise endorsed by the city council, the planning commission, or some other formal body.

For any visioning process, the real challenge is to translate the broad visions that result from this process into specific actions. It's one thing to agree on the need for affordable housing; it's quite another to site a congregate home. But, for many communities, the process of going through a visioning effort helps smooth the way to political consensus. It does so by involving a much broader spectrum of community interests and stakeholders.

Interest-Based Consensus Building. Communities have used task forces and advisory committees for some time. However, some communities are beginning to appoint citizen task forces or advisory bodies on the basis of group interest rather than on the basis of planning subject or neighborhood area. For instance, committees may be made up of those representing the interests of the business community, conservationists, preservationists, working people, developers and contractors, children, senior citizens, and many others. In other words, instead of creating "balanced" task forces on the subjects of, say, land use, water quality, or

A Citizen Participation Sampler

Goals & Objectives for Balanced Growth, Nantucket Planning & Economic Development Commission (1989-1991):

Groups of children, developers, conservationists, renters, harbor workers, employers, seniors, and large land owners each met separately in their own homes to list their "prouds" and "sorries," and to draw "utopian" and "realistic" maps of the future. The planning commission had been allowed to appoint only one convener for each group; conveners could appoint anyone they wanted but were urged to recruit "new blood." Planning commission members were asked to stop planning for a year, sit on the sidelines, and just listen. Each group presented and discussed their findings before cable TV cameras. The findings became the basis for a 48-page growth policy document later adopted by Town Meeting.

traffic congestion—each made up of representatives of a number of interests—there might be one study group composed of only developers, another of people who rent their homes, and one of just transit advocates. The newer interest group processes mark a departure from older styles and structures in that they (a) turn over some authority to groups that stand outside the traditional power structure, and (b) allow emotional and extremist positions to play out before they reach the larger group. The success or failure of this method depends upon the degree to which such groups can find common ground when they come together near the end of the process.

Private Initiatives. Another trend is the increasing involvement of private organizations. Processes are beginning to be conceived, organized, and sponsored by business consortia and nonprofits. At the state level, 1000 Friends-type groups are now up and operating in five states, while environmental organizations have moved into the arena in 11 states. At the metropolitan level, private groups, like the Regional Plan Association in New York or Blue Grass Futures in Lexington, are bringing disparate interests to the table. Locally, chambers of commerce, land trusts, and housing advocacy groups have stepped up to the plate. The bad news is that these efforts may be a reflection of the public's lack of confidence in the public sector's ability to go beyond politics to get the job done. The good news is that the emergence of such efforts is testimony to the value of planning—that thinking about a community's long-range future is simply good business.

Neighborhood Advocacy. Neighborhood-based organizations are beginning to gain access to the tools that they need in order to play a meaningful role in the planning process. Some of the most successful attempts to empower sub-city districts have involved concerted public efforts to organize and train local groups about how to participate. Places like Birmingham, Denver, and Portland have stood out as positive examples. Birmingham officially sponsored 86 separate neighborhood associations—a system that was intended to function as one of the most intensive citizen participation programs operating in the nation. With financial assistance from private corporations, Denver has published the 190-page *Denver Neighborhood Self-Help Guide*. Intended to be a companion document to the Planning Office's *Neighborhood Planning Guide*, it was prepared to assist neighborhood and community organizations to address a variety of issues that affect their property and quality of life. Portland maintains an Office of Neighborhood Associations which acts as a facilitator agency, working to coordinate and assist neighborhood groups.

Charettes: Expert Swat Teams. Bringing in outside experts for a short period is often the jump start that is needed to get a community participation effort moving. A full range of ideas is inventoried; fresh new perspectives are added to the pot. These experts often bring stature and credibility to a bogged down process. Groups that have been known to go to a place to look at a problem and quickly offer solutions include the following:

American Institute of Architects
American Society of Landscape Architects
Institute for Urban Design
International Downtown Association
National Main Street Center
Partners for Livable Places
Project for Public Spaces
Waterfront Center
International Countryside Stewardship Exchange

The charette format is being embraced by others outside the nonprofit sector. Consultants, for instance, will often use a charette format to get a project off the ground. It can serve to educate the project team about community attitudes, desires, and preferences. The more successful attempts have relied heavily on visual imagery to stimulate discussion. In the past several years, visual preference tests have been used to spark community visioning processes.

For the local planner, the use of outside experts for short-term idea blitzes is a useful catalyst. Most of the time, the experts end up making the same points the planner has been trying to get across for years. Hearing it again from out-of-towners sometimes gives the message added credence.

It must be remembered, however, that charettes should never replace a more leisurely paced, methodical, and thoughtful long-range community involvement process. Charettes might be best used to shake a community by the shoulders from time to time to generate fresh thinking about a problem.

A Citizen Participation Sampler

Office of Neighborhood Associations, Portland, Oregon (1974-present)

ONA has evolved into one of the most comprehensive public involvement systems in the nation. Over 90 percent of the city is covered by over 60 private neighborhood associations—all of them linked and supported by five ONA district offices. The offices set up neighborhood meetings and workshops, publish neighborhood association newsletters, provide technical and referral services, produce news releases, and conduct community studies. They also become involved with neighborhood crime prevention programs, code and license review, emergency assistance, budget advisory committees, and needs reporting.

Community Planning Centers. A storefront or other location where citizens can meet to develop plans, examine maps and data, and convene to discuss goals and objectives helps deal with the problem of geographic isolation. Residents and business owners find that participation is enhanced by not having to go downtown to an unfamiliar and somewhat threatening venue. For instance, in Boston, decentralized offices were used during the planning of the Southwest Corridor project—a project to design a major new transit line through low-income neighborhoods. Local people could drop in at their leisure to review plans and register their concerns or ideas about the project.

Technology. The use of local-access cable channels to cover citizen participation events like workshops, charettes, and hearings has been employed more and more across the nation. Interactive television has been somewhat limited in its application to date, although call-in shows on local access TV are more prevalent. The promise of technological enhancement to facilitate meaningful citizen participation is very exciting. There is no doubt that we will see major strides in this area over the next 20 years.

Advances in computer graphics capabilities, data handling, and simulation technology are also very exciting. The ability to animate alternative futures and to create images of hypothetical forms and patterns of development should have very positive implications for citizen participation.

Reaching Into the Citizen Participation Tool Box

There are many techniques that may be employed to increase the effectiveness of citizen participation in the planning and community development process. Some of them have been described above.

Citizen participation constructs are clearly not a "one size fits all" proposition. Tools must be selected, adapted, and configured to meet the unique needs of each region, community, or neighborhood. When fitting these techniques to the needs of low-income and minority neighborhoods, experience has told us that it is important to keep in mind various blocks to success. Racism, paternalism, and resistance to power redistribution on behalf of the majority power structure are often strong impediments to meaningful participation in low-income and minority areas. Impediments on the other side of the equation include inadequate knowledge about the process, inadequate language skills,

---

A Citizen Participation Sampler

Citywide General Plan Framework, City of Los Angeles, California (1993)

The second largest city in the country, where school district students speak 85 languages, will involve residents in this major undertaking through the use of multilingual communication, cable television, one-on-one interviews, bilingual video kits, and child care offerings.

and trouble organizing accountable and representative citizens groups in the face of futility, alienation, and distrust.

There is more art than science in this craft. Veterans indicate that the golden rule continues to be: Let the citizenry play a role in crafting the citizen participation process.

The following represents a master checklist of tools that can be used to craft a good citizen participation program. The items on the list are intended to be selected, mixed, matched, and adapted to the unique political, social, and economic conditions of the locality.

Citizen attitude surveys
Use of mediator or facilitator
Citizen honoraria
Circuit rider services
Citizen training
Citizen representation on boards
Direct funding to community groups
Telephone hotlines
Interactive cable TV
Ombudsman
Open door policy
Visioning sessions
Task forces
Public hearings
Workshops and charettes
Visual preference testing
Topical conference
Neighborhood planning council
Media-based issue balloting
Game simulations
Citizen employment
Citizen advisory board
Media and public information campaigns
Community planning centers

SUMMARY AND CONCLUSIONS

Planners should be mindful of a number of major points concerning approaches to citizen involvement in urban America in the 1990s and beyond:

1.   The meaningful and continuous involvement of local residents and business people during the planning for the revitalization of older, distressed urban neighborhoods must be a *high priority.*

2.   To this end, it is clear that the *old styles* of citizen participation are *not serving us well* in the 1990s.

3.   Some newer techniques developed recently show promise for *adaptation* to the needs of these special neighborhoods.

4.   *New techniques* need to be developed as well.

5.   Planners should take a *leading role* in adapting and creating public participation paradigms for distressed urban areas. However, the forms and patterns of involvement must never be imposed from outside; they must be developed *in partnership with affected neighborhoods.*

6.   Planners should be *bold and innovative* in selecting, adapting, and inventing public involvement mechanisms. They should use their best powers of persuasion to convince decision makers to *take risks* in their community involvement ventures—to dare to share control and authority to get beyond the public hearing mentality of years past.

7.   Planners must begin to develop ways to *evaluate the success or failure* of citizen participation efforts after programs have been completed.

8.   Planners should continue to advocate for better *state statutes* governing planning and the management of change. Modernized statutes should include thoughtful and practical community involvement requirements. They should also contain elements of vertical and horizontal integration that protect the participatory interests of the less fortunate by dealing effectively with the issues of regional fair-share housing, jobs/housing balance, NIMBYs, and LULUs.

The processes developed in this manner will enable the beneficiaries of revitalization efforts to have more of an ownership stake in the process and in the outcomes, and, consequently, more of a say in determining the future character of these neighborhoods.

Bill Klein is director of research for the American Planning Association in Chicago.

10

Governance

By Arnold Cogan, AICP, and Richard RuBino

INTRODUCTION

The old motto, "That government is best which governs least," still raises a major question today. Given the multiplicity of redundant or overlapping special service districts and numerous cities, counties, and other governing bodies, the natural question arises: "Do we have more local government than we need or are willing to support?" As Edmund Burke said, "Government is a contrivance of human wisdom to provide for human wants." When evaluating the conditions of local governance at the end of the 20th century, we should ideally be guided by a knowledge of the nature of human wants and needs.

One major need is equity. In many of America's metropolitan centers, there is a growing gulf between the inner cities and the suburbs. Inequities in the distribution of housing, schools, and type and quality of jobs are causing widening gaps between winners and losers. Growing poverty, crime, and despair in the inner cities impose increasing demands on community resources while revenue-generating activity and employment move into the suburbs and beyond. Establishing equity throughout metropolitan areas is a major challenge to planning; to be successful there must be tangible benefits for all parts of a metropolitan area.

Lesser populated regions also have problems of governance. Many rural regions face the challenge of coping with economic stagnation, population loss, and sometimes just survival. Add unanticipated natural onslaughts, such as the disastrous storms and floods of 1993-1994, and many undercapitalized and ill-equipped smaller regions become overwhelmed.

Despite differences in geography and political traditions, all regions face similar problems. Political balkanization, unguided growth, leap-frogging development, and competition for infrastructure, schools, and economic development are but a few of the problems that touch nearly every entity. These complex, often interconnected problems demand inventive approaches to resolving them.

Finally, the dilemmas and challenges of leadership must be considered, particularly the natural reluctance of politicians to transgress on some-one else's turf—to suggest solutions outside one's own jurisdiction. Despite Neal Peirce's caution that constituents will not support "coordi-nated government," planning must generate future leaders who will devote their energies to collaboration of people across political bound-aries. Planners must nurture people willing to work together to achieve reform in governance. And planners must be among these future leaders.

The vision of most Americans, according to Anthony Downs, is to retain strong control over local governance, drive their cars to work, and live in low-density, semi-rural surroundings. In a narrow, self-serving sense, many people seemed to benefit from the pursuit of this vision. But even the winners are beginning to feel some discomfort, as crime, juvenile pregnancy, and scourges such as AIDS reach out to even the most pristine suburbs. The pursuit of the American dream is becoming too expensive to support in terms of infrastructure, damage to the environment, and social and political dysfunctions.

Governance must be part of the solution, rather than a contributor to the problem. There can be no change unless governments themselves begin to change. They must learn to work more cooperatively and less competitively than in the past. This change is beginning to occur. This paper outlines some of these changes and closes with the suggestion that planners can address the problems of equity more effectively by facilitating communicative and collaborative governance.

PRESCRIPTIONS FOR DEALING WITH DIFFICULT ISSUES

Political Environment

Most local decision makers deal with issues on a piecemeal basis within their own jurisdictions, isolated from other units of government. They willingly or unwillingly fail to take into account impacts on neighboring communities or the region as a whole. Housing, social services, public safety, public health, land use, economic development, transportation, water supply, and revenue generation require solutions that stretch beyond boundaries of most local governments. Each of these would benefit from collaborative approaches that integrate local priorities into regionwide perspectives.

This era of budget cutbacks and shrinking public spending may have an unanticipated benefit: a pragmatic need to achieve a more satisfactory balance of resources within metropolitan (and even rural) regions. Fiscal disparities and uneven delivery of services among local units of government create a need to minimize tax inequities, redistribute revenues more fairly, fund human service functions more adequately, and generally create a more equitable socioeconomic balance among the haves and have-nots.

With the exception of ISTEA (Intermodal Surface Transportation Efficiency Act of 1991), the innovative federal approach to funding transportation projects, financial assistance from federal and state governments has been difficult to come by as local governments confront their own fiscal crises. Alternative approaches to local government modernization, regional collaboration or governance, and integrated local-state partnerships that promote areawide social and economic equity must face these financial realities.

ALTERNATIVE APPROACHES TO NEW GOVERNANCE

A wave of activity leading to collaborative arrangements between local governments, regional entities, and integrated local-state partnerships is sweeping the country. It is not yet a massive wave, but experimental activities are surfacing everywhere—in metropolitan regions like New York City and San Antonio and in places like the rural areas of Iowa and Kansas. These experiments may be the seedlings of reform that will allow governments to more capably address problems that have been unresolved largely because of governmental competition and divisiveness.

Most of the new intergovernmental collaborations deal with basic issues such as transportation, water supply, and environmental protection. However, imaginative intergovernmental experiments also are surfacing in programs that more directly confront social equity issues like affordable housing.

Local Government Modernization

Though retaining control over local governance remains a dominant vision in every part of the country, local governance is being modernized through both internal and external changes. The internal transformation is reflected in the movement toward neighborhood empowerment in urban areas. As Peirce and Guskind illustrate in *Breakthroughs*, the political power of organized neighborhoods is "re-creating the American city." Examples of neighborhood empowerment include Boston's southwest corridor; the radial reuse plan in Lincoln, Nebraska; self-help in Cabrillo Village, California; and bridge relocation in Seattle.

The external changes are revealed by the increasing number of cooperative unions being formed with other local governments or levels of government. We are finding that working together strengthens local governance. Working together represents a spirit of new governance.

External changes take several forms: some are initiated by local governments themselves, while others are precipitated by mandates from federal or state governments. The major categories of externally oriented modernization are interlocal agreements, transfer of selected services to special districts, transfer or assumption of selected services from one form of general purpose local government to another, and consolidation or unification.

Voluntary interlocal agreements. Voluntary interlocal agreements are not new but they are taking on added popularity. This activity is stimulated by the need to find alternative means to providing services previously assisted through federal aid. In an article in *Governing*, Eileen Shanahan observed that: "local governments everywhere are joining together, at an accelerating pace, to deal with the ever-increasing variety of problems that defy solution within established political boundaries." Planning is a fundamental component of many of these

> ## Collaborative planning efforts can, and do, work
>
> When one looks across today's American cityscape, there are exceptions to urban mediocrity, discouragement and complacency: collaborative city planning efforts that can, and do, work; housing programs that can function without being throttled by bureaucracy; local governments that bend themselves into new shapes and forms to accommodate their citizens; a revived city market or new urban plaza that is a joy to walk through; schools that ignite a love of learning, of possibility, in their students; police systems that treat citizens more as allies than suspects; community-based partnerships that create new housing and new enterprises even when government agencies claim it cannot be done. (Peirce and Guskind 1993)

"joinings." Thus, a growing demand for greater efficiency in providing services is coupled to a dawning awareness that local governments are no longer islands unto themselves.

A promising experiment is underway in Connecticut. The Connecticut Regional Housing Policy Act of 1988 triggered pilot programs to achieve voluntary regional compacts for fair share housing programs in both the Hartford and Bridgeport regions. The Capital Region Council of Governments successfully negotiated a compact that overcame the Not in My Back Yard mentality by getting 26 communities to agree to increase opportunities for affordable housing. The compact is built around three principles: Each community is to put forth its "best effort" to meet its shortfall in affordable housing, financially support the effort to the extent possible, and adopt from a list of possible implementation strategies those most appropriate to its situation. The Bridgeport area has adopted a similar program. These are pilot programs, but if they prove successful they will be breakthroughs for addressing equity issues on a regional basis.

Urban governments from one side of the nation to the other are entering voluntary interlocal agreements in an attempt to better contend with the consequences of urban sprawl. New York City, with the assistance of the Regional Plan Association, is forging interlocal partnerships with 75 rural communities in its three upstate watersheds to support improved land management in those watersheds. Down in

Texas, the San Antonio Water System is undertaking a negotiated water resource planning program among the multiple users of the Edwards Aquifer. The program is a cooperative, intergovernmental effort funded by county governments and municipalities, and will require extensive, collaborative planning.

In Palm Beach County, Florida, the Municipal League got local governments to establish a countywide clearinghouse through which all municipal and county planning amendments are circulated for the review and comment of other local governments. On the West Coast, the San Francisco Bay Area Partnership is meeting to find ways of financing innovative answers to transportation needs in the metropolitan area.

The interest in interlocal agreements is not restricted to urban areas. Fifteen towns in upstate New York work together under the Cooperative Tug Hill Council to guide development in the region. The municipalities share two planning circuit riders, and six of the communities have formed a cooperative zoning board of appeals. Similar cooperative approaches are being considered by the tier counties in New York State and in eastern Pennsylvania. Agreements leading to clustering of rural communities in Iowa and Kansas allow for sharing of services and tax bases.

According to Tim Borich of Iowa State University, many communities throughout the Midwest are in the process of interconnecting their planning, service provision, and economic development activities. With the growing inability of farm economies to support village and town main streets, new linkages between communities are materializing. Different and varying levels of community are emerging.

Borich believes that a redefinition of "community" is beginning to take place that improves the social and political environment for intergovernmental collaboration. He also argues that when collaboration takes place, it is usually on a scale that allows participating rural governments to continue to have a major influence on regional decisions. Within this context, rural governments may deal with the emerging reality of economic transition and growing interdependency while maintaining some degree of autonomy.

Innovative interlocal agreements are emerging in the rural West, too. For example, in Arizona, the state chapter of the American Planning

Association is exploring improved coordination between the Salt River Pima-Maricopa Indian Community and surrounding local governments.

Transfer of selected services to special purpose districts. Creating special purpose districts has long been and continues to be the most popular way to provide services on an interjurisdictional basis. Statistics show that they are the most rapidly growing form of local government. Such districts generate their own funds through either property or ad valorem taxes or user fees and usually are not dependent on annual appropriations from a general purpose government.

A critical downside to special districts, however, is that they customarily are governed by appointed bodies not directly accountable to voters. They tend to "disempower" rather than empower the general citizenry and, because of this, are not a preferable form of new governance. It is a paradox that the popularity of special districts continues to soar when citizen participation in governmental matters appears to have become such a high priority. But as local governments seek new and imaginative ways of working together, interest in special districts may begin to slow.

Transfer or assumption of selected services from one form of general purpose local government to another. Another way to restructure is to transfer a responsibility to another local government. County governments are often the recipients of these transfers. Schneider and Park note that because of stringent fiscal limits faced by municipalities, county governments in some urban areas are assuming greater responsibilities for service delivery. In addition, county governments are beginning to play a greater role in ensuring consistency in planning among municipal governments. The Pinellas County, Florida, Planning Council has received national acclaim for its countywide planning consistency program, which requires municipal plans to be consistent with the countywide plan. Comparable consistency requirements exist for municipalities in Broward County (Fort Lauderdale), Florida.

In 1989, the Nevada legislature enacted a law that created, in each county with a population between 100,000 and 400,000, a regional planning commission that must establish guidelines for determining whether municipal master plans and facilities plans conform with the countywide regional plan. Similar action has been taken in Massachusetts, where county governance heretofore has been practically nonexistent. To deal with issues that transcend the boundaries of municipal governments in Barnstable County (Cape Cod), the commonwealth created a charter that placed greater responsibility for planning and development regulation in the hands of county government. This responsibility is operated through the Cape Cod Commission. Legislation is being considered in Pennsylvania to give counties a role in overseeing municipal planning and achieving countywide consistency.

Going it jointly

Service sharing is hot. Outright consolidation is not. In between, governments are finding plenty of other ways to gang up on the demands of the '90s. The most common, and the most rapidly growing, form of regionalism in government, however, consists of simple agreements to consolidate specific services, cooperate in their provision, or shift their provision from one government to another. (Shanahan 1991)

Consolidation or unification. The most complete form of local government reform is consolidation. This is customarily discussed in terms of city-county consolidations, but it can also apply to mergers of cities, villages, and/or townships. Between 1980 and 1990, three city-county consolidations were formed: Athens-Clarke County, Georgia; Houma-Terrebonne Parish, Louisiana; and Lynchburg City-Moore County, Tennessee. In addition, consolidations or mergers of communities also occurred in Battle Creek City-Town, Michigan; Willimantic-Windham Township, Connecticut; and Putnam-Putnam Township, Connecticut.

Though none of these consolidations took place in densely populated metropolitan areas, all but one were in urbanizing areas. Consolidation took place in Battle Creek because the Kellogg Corporation threatened to move its corporate headquarters elsewhere unless the habitually competing governments of the city and township consolidated. Representatives of Kellogg said that the competition among divided communities not only cost the company unnecessary taxes, but bickering between the governments also created an unhealthy climate for economic development.

Another factor leading to consolidation is the rapid urbanization of formerly rural townships and counties. The two mergers in Connecticut resulted in urban townships suburban to Hartford and other nearby urban centers. Thus, despite the absence of consolidations of a grander scale, such as occurred in Indianapolis-Marion County a decade earlier, merger of small local governments on the fringes of urbanizing areas holds promise for helping inadequately sized communities trying to cope with the costly demands of rapid growth.

Consolidation or unification also might provide a more direct approach to problems of equity. Through appropriate forms of representation or districting, minority interests might exert more lasting impact on equity problems in the framework of a consolidated government than minority controlled legislatures operating in independent but balkanized and resource-weak inner cities. This may be a touchy issue, but in the pursuit of equity it is worthy of debate.

Regional Collaboration or Governance

Mention regional governance and the drawbridge protecting the castle of local democracy is immediately raised. "Regionalism is as welcome most places as a rash," quips Neal Peirce. Yet, despite the truth of this witticism, he and others continue to expound on a need for regionalism. Occasional progress is made, but the trail is rife with pitfalls.

Regional planning agencies, halfway houses to regionalism, remain the most popular form of regional cooperation, because they most commonly are advisory, not policy-making, bodies. They represent what can be called "stage one" regionalism, guaranteed not to create a significant threat to the status quo. Local governments rarely have to abide by regional plans, and few regional planning agencies can do more than point out the consequences of extravagant urbanization.

In an effort to improve their relevance in intergovernmental affairs, many regional planning agencies are experimenting with a new role: that of consensus-building. Under Florida's recently amended growth management laws, all regional planning agencies are required to assist local governments in resolving planning conflicts; thus, the agencies are assuming roles as facilitators to resolve local governmental disputes.

However, Douglas Porter, in a paper discussing coordination of transportation and land-use planning, argues that more than just facilitating negotiations is necessary for effective metropolitan management of land use. Two of the keys he discusses regarding management of land use may apply equally to regional governance: forming a metropolitan vision and defining a metropolitan constituency.

Visions are relatively easy to come by, but defining a metropolitan constituency is a major weakness for most regional planning agencies. Counties have constituencies, therefore utilizing counties for management of land use may be more realistic than creating some new form of regional governance. However, the strong urban county model is not appropriate in multicounty metropolitan areas. In highly metropolitanized areas, inventing a new structure that requires local governments to define and serve a different constituency requires political courage and leadership seldom forthcoming. But it has been done.

Stage two regionalism goes beyond providing advisory and technical planning services and establishes mandatory regional policies or operates regionwide services. This is exemplified by the Twin Cities Metropolitan Council and the Portland, Oregon, Metro (formerly the Metropolitan Service District.) The Metropolitan Council is a quasi-governmental body that covers a seven-county area and operates a number of regionwide programs. It reviews community planning for conformance with the regional plan, oversees agencies such as the Metropolitan Waste Control Commission, and is particularly noted for its tax base sharing program. A portion of the revenues collected annually from the commercial and industrial tax base of each local government is redistributed according to regionally determined needs.

The Portland Metro covers the urbanized portion of a three-county area. Unlike the Twin Cities Council, whose members are appointed by the governor, Metro is governed by an elected council and an executive officer who is elected regionwide. It operates the region's solid waste and recycling program, a zoo, and convention and cultural facilities. The service district also is responsible for regional transportation planning, urban growth management, natural areas, water resource management, and economic development.

These successful examples notwithstanding, most of America is satisfied with stage one regionalism—regionalism that does not radically tamper with the status quo. David Pampu of the Denver Regional Council of Governments suggests tampering with a different level of status quo. He suggests that we refocus our thinking on moving authorities from the state level to the metropolitan level.

The federal ISTEA program could be used as a model to move some aspects of environmental protection, including air and water quality, and certain social service activities closer to the people. Other new forms of regionalism are also being discussed in California, which is struggling to find a politically acceptable means of consolidating fractionated regional services.

Local-State Partnerships

A third approach to new governance involves the integrated management of functional responsibilities between local and state governments. A wide variety of functions is affected: environmental regulation, solid waste siting, 911 systems, and growth management, for example. In the last 20 years, integrated growth management systems have been instituted in Florida, Georgia, Maine, New Jersey, Oregon, Rhode Island, Vermont, and Washington. More are being considered (e.g., Maryland, Massachusetts, Michigan, Pennsylvania, Virginia).

To one degree or another, these growth management systems have influenced or required changes in local governance. Each has required its local governments to plan, and, in most instances, to elevate the priority of intergovernmental, especially interlocal, relationships. Requirements for local governments to communicate with each other during the planning process have resulted not only in improved coordination but in other collaborative arrangements, as well. According to Chet Mattson, director of the Bergen County, New Jersey, planning department, the cross-acceptance process, whereby local governments within a county are required to exchange drafts of their plans, has resulted in neighboring communities reaching interlocal agreements to share costs and provision of services they otherwise would not have discussed.

Intergovernmental cooperation through state-mandated growth management is one thing, but in Florida, a state reputed to have a top-down approach to growth management, a more experimental approach is being taken. A special 1993 act created the South Walton Development and Conservation Trust, a collaborative local-state venture in planning. The trust, half of whose members are appointed by the county commission and the other half by the governor, is preparing a plan for a highly desirable, yet relatively undeveloped coastal area in south Walton County. The county is interested in the local benefits to be gained from developing the area, whereas the state is concerned about the preservation of fragile and pristine coastal resources. Together, they are developing a plan that will balance and benefit both interests. This experiment in local-state collaboration may prove to be a new model of governance in Florida and elsewhere.

CHALLENGE TO PLANNERS

Solutions to our nation's social inequities are confounded by the growing disparities between inner cities and more well-to-do suburbs, edge cities, and exurbs. A major obstacle to resolving social inequities is governance, especially in regard to structural issues, tax policies, and interjurisdictional linkages. To these factors may be added the question of how to empower neighborhoods while developing areawide constituencies. Another question of scale is that of balancing decision making on local issues with effective ways to deal with metropolitan or areawide needs.

As leaders in addressing problems of social inequities, planners must be attuned to the changes that are possible and be willing to devise and apply prescriptions that meet the needs of their metropolitan areas or rural regions. A primary goal should be to develop effective forms of new governance that can resolve the critical problems of social inequities along with those of economic opportunity and environmental protection.

In support of this goal, planners must work to:

- Empower neighborhoods to act democratically and responsively.

- Provide opportunities and access for all citizens to have meaningful participation in the process of reforming governance.

- Facilitate intergovernmental collaborations.

- Achieve equitable distribution and broader focus of power and resources between financially deprived inner cities and more well-to-do suburbs through changes in governance.

• Improve fiscal balance among local governments by mitigating fiscal disparities.

• Expedite regional consensus on areawide issues.

• Consolidate or unify local entities or functions.

Armed with areawide perspectives and consensus building skills, planners must work toward building constituencies that understand the need for changes in local governance and develop a will to act. Planners throughout the country are already contributing to collaborative intergovernmental programs. Yet even more needs to be done in addressing the needs of social equity and achievement of greater fiscal balance in both metropolitan and rural areas. To do this, and to facilitate cooperation among people across political boundaries, planners must play leadership roles.

The need for new governance can no longer be ignored; it must be placed high on the agenda of planners. Planners in both urban and rural areas already have played major roles in facilitating intergovernmental collaboration and in creating other forms of new governance. Above all, today's motto should be that government is best when done collaboratively.

BIBLIOGRAPHY

Borich, Timothy. 1993. From a memorandum to Mary Kihl, Iowa State University, Ames, Iowa, November 11, 1993.

Breckenfeld, Gary. 1982. "Kellogg's Battle of Battle Creek," *Fortune*, November 29, 1982.

Downs, Anthony. 1989. *The Need for a New Vision for the Development of Large U.S. Metropolitan Areas*. New York: Salomon Brothers.

Mattson, Chester. From a presentation on a panel titled "Planning and the Sharing of Power," National Conference of the American Planning Association, Chicago, May 4, 1992.

Nolan, John. 1909. "What is Needed in American City Planning?" Proceedings of the First National Conference on City Planning (Washington, DC, May 21-22, 1909), Chicago: American Society of Planning Officials, 1967.

Pampu, David A. 1993. From a letter to Arnold Cogan, Portland, Ore., from Denver, Colo., November 17, 1993.

Peirce, Neal. 1991. "Regional Governance: Why? Now? How?" *University of Virginia Newsletter*, June 1991.

Peirce, Neal R., and Robert Guskind. 1993. *Breakthroughs: Re-creating the American City*. New Brunswick, N.J.: Center for Urban Policy Research, Rutgers University.

Porter, Douglas R. 1991. *Transportation, Urban Form, and the Environment.* Washington, D.C.: Transportation Research Board, National Research Council.

Schneider, Mark, and Kee Ok Park. 1989. "Metropolitan Counties as Service Delivery Agents: The Still Forgotten Governments," *Public Administration Review* 49, 4: 345-352.

Shanahan, Eileen. 1991. "Going It Jointly: Regional Solutions for Local Problems," *Governing* 4, 11: 70-76.

Wheeler, Michael. 1993. "Regional Consensus on Affordable Housing: Yes in My Backyard?" *Journal of Planning Education and Research* 12, 2: 139-149.

Arnold Cogan is the managing partner of Cogan Owens Cogan, planning and public affairs consultants, a registered professional engineer, member of the American Institute of Certified Planners (AICP), and immediate past chair of the APA Intergovernmental Affairs Division. He is a specialist in public involvement, project management, governmental relations, policy, and land-use planning. Richard G. RuBino is an associate professor of urban and regional planning at Florida State University and is current chairman of APA's Intergovernmental Affairs Division. He has directed Vermont's Planning Office and has done local government consulting in Illinois, Missouri, and Pennsylvania.

11

Capital Improvements and Equity

By William Lucy, AICP

A capital improvements program (CIP) is a financial instrument for scheduling project costs and debt service and limiting fluctuations. It typically covers five or six years. A CIP is a priority planning instrument for implementing elements of comprehensive plans, development plans, and functional plans. It also is an instrument for distributing projects geographically. In these ways, capital improvement programs operationalize the concept of equity.[1]

Equity is concerned with what is fair. Equity evokes eternal questions about "who should get what." Spontaneous responses to that question often take the form of saying "everyone should get the same facilities and services." But for some services that is impossible, and sometimes it is undesirable when it is possible. If some people need more of certain services than others, equity may call for unequal rather than equal service distribution.

In this paper, I will examine the implications of five concepts of equity for answering the question, "Who should get what?" I will consider the role of planning standards, stages of planning processes during which planners can apply the equity concepts, indicators of facility and service distribution, and methods of rating priorities in capital improvement programming.

EQUALITY

One equity notion is that everyone should receive the same facilities unless there are "good" reasons to do something else. In practice, equality may be impossible, as when physical facilities are involved. Some facilities, like parks, libraries, fire stations, and bus stops are generally considered good things to be near. But because they are few in number, people will inevitably be located at varying distances from them. In such instances, an equality standard is constructed as a threshold of adequacy, so that everyone should be within an acceptable distance of the facility in order to obtain service when they need or want it.

Many facilities, however, are considered bad for their neighbors, even though they may be good, even essential, for the community. Examples of such facilities are toxic waste disposal sites, halfway houses, and expressway interchanges. In these instances, an equality standard

---

Defining the CIP

To refresh the memories of those whose only exposure to a CIP was in a textbook, it is a multi-year schedule of public physical improvements. . . . The CIP sets forth proposed expenditures for systematically constructing, maintaining, upgrading, and replacing a community's physical plant. Capital improvement projects are typically major, infrequent expenditures, such as the construction of a new facility or nonrecurring rehabilitation or major repair of an existing facility.

For a planner, a CIP is more than a schedule of expenditures. [L]ike any budgetary process, a CIP is also riddled with policy issues, choices, and political pressures. The policy issues are often unwritten or unstated assumptions, but they are a powerful force in driving the program.

Every planner doing a CIP needs to understand that preparing a budget, whether for operating or capital expenditures, is more than technical procedures. A budget is at the heart of the political process. A budget reconciles the conflicts in our democratic society and allocated limited resources among competing interests.

After the political posturing and oratory are over, it is a test of how society "puts its money where its mouth is." . . . Invariably, a budget is a set of compromises reflecting political accommodation.

—Robert A. Bowyer, AICP, *Capital Improvements Programs: Linking Budgeting and Planning*, PAS Report Number 442, 1993.

would call for avoiding cumulative disadvantages, in which one neighborhood would have many of these undesirable facilities while other neighborhoods have none.

NEED

Need is the opposite of equality, in that it implies that unequals should be treated in an appropriately unequal manner based on relevant reasons. Relevant reasons connect individual characteristics, territorial features, and the purposes for which public facilities and services are provided.

Need indicators can be general or specific. Poverty is a general need indicator; persons in poverty will have little capacity to pay for private goods and services, such as books and recreation. Proximity to a public library and recreation center would be a greater need for poverty families than for well-to-do families. The importance of a governmental response to needs of persons in poverty is especially apparent when large poverty concentrations occur, as they often do.

Need indicators also can be specifically relevant to public functions. Structural conditions associated with high fire incidence, and fire-related injuries and deaths, would indicate need for a fire station nearby so that response time to reported fires would be brief.

DEMAND

The notion of basing equity on demand implies that active interest by constituents in a service should be rewarded. Belief in the appropriateness of responding to citizen concerns is a fundamental principle of democratic governance. Demand for local facilities and services is expressed either in use of services or in requests and complaints about them. It seems sensible to respond to requests for service and to avoid forcing a service on reluctant consumers.

But conflicts occur between demand and other equity concepts. Take libraries, for example. If use—manifested in book circulation rates—is relied on to allocate funds for acquiring library materials, determining hours of operation, remodeling aging structures, and even locating additional branches, middle- and upper-income neighborhoods usually will be the beneficiaries. But such a planning standard would conflict both with basing equity on need (poverty) and equality (everyone should be no greater distance than some mileage threshold from similar facilities).

Residents of better-off neighborhoods may register more requests for improved service, such as for public school improvements, refurbished parks, and reconstructed streets, than do residents of poorer neighborhoods. In such instances, the democratic ideal of responsiveness may lead to unequal distribution of public investments contrary to the distribution that need indicators would produce.

PREFERENCE

Preferences supplement demands. Preferences may be unexpressed, either because access to facilities is difficult, thereby limiting use, or because constituents are inarticulate or skeptical about the results if they were to make requests or complaints. But the means of ascertaining preferences, including public hearings, committees, and surveys, are inaccurate or expensive. They also may yield results at odds with equality and need approaches to equitable distributions of capital facilities.

WILLINGNESS TO PAY

A common equity idea is that people who use a service should pay for it. The amount of use then is determined by willingness (and ability) to pay for it. This principle is applied most often with services for which units can be purchased and billed incrementally. Utility services—water, sewer, gas, and electricity—to individual structures usually are financed this way. Some discretionary services, like public transit and specialized recreation programs, often are billed to users. Emergency services like police and fire, developmental services like education and libraries, and amenity services, like neighborhood parks, rarely are charged to individual users.

When willingness to pay is used to finance a service, partial use of other equity concepts still may occur. Fares almost always are supplemented from the general fund in financing public transit, thereby taking need into account. In addition, demand influences the location of routes. Gas and electricity use may not be subsidized directly, but generous delays in shutting off service during cold weather and special funds to help those unable to pay their bills invoke the need concept of equity. So even when willingness to pay is emphasized, it often is modified by other equity concepts.

The most questionable application of the willingness to pay concept occurs when it is applied to the initial provision of facilities and services, as through special assessments on users to have services installed. Sometimes, entire neighborhoods may be excluded from water and sewer service because residents are unable to pay the cost of connections, even if they can pay for small amounts of the service once it is connected.

STAGES IN APPLYING EQUITY CONCEPTS

Three stages are useful for applying equity concepts to capital improvement programming. In the first stage, the implications of using equity concepts other than equality should be considered. In the second stage, estimates of the distributional consequences of the jurisdiction's current planning standards should be made. In the third stage, alternative equity concepts for specific facilities and services should be discussed with decision makers.

This order is suggested to limit analytical efforts and deliberation costs. The first stage involves brainstorming and does not require research. The second stage requires determining what distributional planning standards and decision rules have been used, and are currently being used, for capital improvements, and some analysis of the actual consequences of their use. The third stage involves capturing the attention of key decision makers and deliberating with them about whether they are willing to change the balance among equity concepts, or whether the political costs of confrontation with them should be engaged.

In stage two, consequences of planning standards for facilities and decision rules for services should be identified by analyzing patterns of facility and service distribution. An analytic framework with examples of indicators is presented in the following table. This framework is a version of a systems analysis. It includes indicators of resources (facilities, equipment, expenditures, and personnel) and activities (measured by frequency and duration) which have direct results (including intended and unintended consequences) and secondary impacts (changes in social conditions, which usually have multiple causes).

EXAMPLES OF FACILITY AND SERVICE INDICATORS

RESOURCES	Facilities	Neighborhood park acres per 1,000 residents, fire stations and branch libraries per 10,000 residents
	Equipment	Playground swings per 1,000 children age 12 and under
	Expenditures	Dollars per 1,000 persons or 1,000 households for neighborhood parks and playgrounds, branch libraries, and fire and police stations
	Personnel	Number per 1,000 persons or 1,000 households for branch library operations, neighborhood park maintenance, and water line repair
ACTIVITIES	Frequency	Refuse pick-ups per week, street cleanings per month, hours of operation of swimming pools and branch libraries per week, time between buses (headways)
	Duration	Response time by police and fire personnel from receipt of call for service, and speed of repairs, such as average length of interrupted water and sewer service for repairs
RESULTS	Intended Consequences	Satisfactory water pressure at the tap, satisfactory street bumpiness ratings, satisfactory fire suppression rates, residents sufficiently satisfied with neighborhood parks and other services in citizen surveys
	Unintended Consequences	Days of unpleasant water taste, number of missed refuse collections, residents dissatisfied with the quantity or quality of facilities and services in citizen surveys
	Use of Service, by Amount	Library books circulated per year, swimmers per day, park users per week, bus riders per day
	Failure to Use, by Reason	Percent of residents not using bus service due to excessive waits and walking distances, percent of residents not using branch libraries due to distance
IMPACTS	Changes in Social Conditions	Facility and service relationships to social indicators, such as crime rates, property values, satisfaction with neighborhoods, and the like, which are partially identifiable with quasi-experimental design and multivariate statistical analyses

Multiple measures of facilities and services are needed in distributional analyses, because findings using different types of indicators—such as indicators of resources and results—often will yield divergent findings. Equality in expenditures (resource indicators) in parks for basketball courts and lighting may not be matched by equality in amount of use (result indicator) or the condition of facilities and equipment after one year (result indicator). Both types of indicators are important. Public officials also may be interested in crime rate changes (impact indicator) before and after the investment in basketball courts, although impact indicators reflect multiple influences.

PRIORITIES IN CAPITAL IMPROVEMENTS

Because capital improvement programs implement elements of comprehensive plans, development plans, functional plans, and campaign promises, they will be shaped with more than distributional equity in mind. In Philadelphia and Utica, New York, for example, capital improvements were used to advance citywide economic development goals, including constituting the local share of federally supported development projects. In Syracuse, New York, capital improvements were used to redeem mayoral campaign promises to build new schools as part of a pledge to spend more in neighborhoods and less in the central business district.

Capital improvements also implement citywide goals in formal planning processes. In St. Paul, Minnesota, a two-year process included proposals initiated by department heads, business groups, and neighborhood associations, review by a commission composed of district citizen planning councils, public hearings, a recommended capital budget submitted by the mayor, and final decision by the city council.

The participants' options were limited, however, by an allocation policy previously adopted by the city council which assigned percentages of the total allocation to categories, including neighborhood improvement, economic development, and citywide service improvement. Within categories, planners used a complicated rating system, with points assigned to a variety of potential benefits. Ratings included whether each proposed project conformed with the comprehensive plan and with the capital allocations policy, as well as many other considerations.

In Falls Church, Virginia, the city council deliberated about large projects, but also set aside fixed amounts each year for streets, parkland acquisition, utility undergrounding, storm drainage, and economic development. These categories provided funds to take advantage of public-private partnership leveraging opportunities that occurred outside the budget cycle, as well as permitting delegation of detailed priority decisions within previously approved dollar limits to the city manager and department heads.

With formal CIP processes, such as those in St. Paul and Falls Church, deliberations about equity criteria can occur at several stages. Formal CIP processes increase the usefulness of detailed analysis of current and past facility distribution and service quality patterns. It is particularly important to determine whether certain neighborhoods experience cumulative deficiencies. A specific neighborhood may appear disadvantaged in neighborhood park acreage and equipment, for example, but perhaps not sufficiently to warrant locating a new neighborhood park there. But if this same neighborhood also is deficient in distance from library services, fire response time, water quality and pressure, and street, sidewalk, and curb conditions, then remedial action on several of these facilities and services would deserve high priority.

If detailed analyses of facility and service distribution are conducted, mayors, city managers, county administrators, council members, county supervisors, planning commissions, and citizens are empowered to compare services and deliberate about appropriate standards, including equity considerations. Such an analysis was conducted by the City of Savannah. It found predominantly poor and black neighborhoods were underserved with sewers, fire hydrants, and paved streets. After greater attention was paid to these cumulative neighborhood disparities, a subsequent survey found that the infrastructure inequalities had been reduced.

CONCLUSION

Geographic distribution of services may not receive enough weight in making capital improvement program decisions. Some evidence on that score is available from an Urban Institute survey of decision processes in 25 cities.

The Urban Institute found that the most frequently used criteria were effects of capital projects on operating and maintenance costs (19 cities), conformance to adopted plans and policies (16), availability of state or federal funds (14), health and safety effects (13), geographic distribution effects (10), economic revitalization effects (10), existing substandard or emergency situations (9), environmental or aesthetic effects (8), legal mandates (7), operational efficiency (7), departmental priorities (6), energy conservation (5), elected officials' priorities (5), and outside pressure (5).

It is unfortunate that only 10 of 25 cities used geographic distribution effects in making CIP decisions. Especially in large and populous jurisdictions, failure to take geographic distribution of facilities and services into account can lead to severe inequities.

NOTES

1. For additional discussion of the relationship between capital improvements and equity, see William Lucy, *Close to Power: Setting Priorities with Elected Officials* (Chapter 5, Capital Budgeting and Priority Planning, and Chapter 7, Equity Concepts and Priority Planning), Chicago: Planners Press, 1988; Lucy, "Equity Planning for Infrastructure: Applications" in Jay M. Stein, ed., *Public Infrastructure Planning and Management*, Beverly Hills: Sage Publications, 1988; and Frank S. Levy, Arnold J. Meltsner, and Aaron Wildavsky, *Urban Outcomes*, Berkeley: University of California Press, 1974.

William H. Lucy, AICP, is professor of Urban and Environmental Planning at the University of Virginia. He is author of Close to Power: Setting Priorities with Elected Officials, *1988, Planners Press. His current research addresses explanations of why both central cities and many suburbs have been declining.*

The University's Role in Community Development

By Elva E. Tillman

For the most part, institutions of higher learning have traditionally been viewed as "academic" in their approach to community development. The second college edition of *The American Heritage Dictionary* appropriately describes that approach in its definition of the term:

> Relating to studies that are liberal or classical rather than technical or vocational . . . Pertaining or belonging to a scholarly organization; scholarly to the point of being unaware of the outside world . . . Theoretical or speculative without a practical purpose or intention. Without purpose or use because of being beyond the point of implementation.

In general, universities are criticized for producing "academic" research not relevant to the realities facing community-based groups and public agencies. But academic institutions can serve a range of roles in the growth and development of our communities. This range of roles must be encouraged at a time when federal and state funding is limited and local alternative financing appears to be minimal. In light of the continued cuts in federal and state community development funds, communities and public agencies need consistent and sustained academic support in their "real-world" efforts. Universities can and do play a range of roles to support the real world. A university can be analyst, consultant, developer (i.e., residential, economic development), researcher,

197

technical-assistance provider and a source of staffing (i.e., internships and permanent jobs).

To stimulate academic institutions to think even more comprehensively about community development issues, this paper endeavors to provide examples of universities and colleges that are undertaking a range of approaches to community development issues. As the Clinton administration advocates more community service, existing federal programs stimulating community involvement are also noted, along with several national nonprofit organizations and private foundations that provide technical assistance and funding to universities and colleges.

Programs of the U.S. Department of Housing and Urban Development (HUD) are emphasized in this article because of HUD's focus on community development issues. Academic institutions should be aware that the U.S. Department of Education also provides funding for community service programs. Other federal agencies, such as the U.S. Department of Health and Human Services, the U.S. Department of Commerce, and the U.S. Department of Transportation, should be consulted for funding relating to specialized aspects of community development. State and local government agencies, as well as national and local foundations and nonprofit organizations can be of assistance in the identification of funding and/or support programs for the cultivation of university community service/development initiatives.

In June 1987, *Planning* magazine included an article, "Class Acts" by Ruth Knack. The article focused on planning programs that had gone through the accreditation process of the Association of Collegiate Schools of Planning (ACSP). Accreditation teams were composed of members from the ACSP, the American Institute of Certified Planners (AICP), and the American Planning Association (APA). Teams that visited the universities were impressed by the fact that the programs were cooperating with community organizations and public agencies to provide "real-world" support from an academic setting.

Of interest are the efforts of: UCLA's Urban Innovations Group; the Center for Community Development and Design, at the University of Colorado at Denver; the Voorhees Center for Neighborhood and Community Improvement and the Center for Urban Economic Development—both at the University of Illinois at Chicago. Also noteworthy

Programs at Historically Black Colleges

Historically black colleges and universities (HBCUs), which grew out of the need in the African American community to prepare freed slaves to assist their communities, have launched impressive community development programs with institutional support. More recently, the U.S. Department of Housing and Urban Development (HUD) has distributed requests for proposals for funding through its technical assistance program and Historically Black Colleges and Universities Cooperative Agreement to: "provide funding for HBCUs who want to take a leading role in addressing local community development needs, including neighborhood revitalization, housing, economic development, etc."

In 1991, HUD made grants to the following HBCUs, to provide a range of technical assistance to their adjacent communities:

Center for Public Affairs, Florida A&M University, Tallahassee.

Economic Development Center of Texas Southern University in Houston.

Center for Technology Transfer, Jackson State University, Jackson, Mississippi.

Institute for Urban Affairs and Research, Howard University, Washington, D.C.

Department of Community Planning and Urban Studies, Alabama A&M University, Huntsville.

Office of Community Development, St. Augustine's College, Raleigh, North Carolina.

Division of Development and Planning, Elizabeth City State University, Elizabeth City, North Carolina.

Community Development Resource Center, Institute for Urban Research at Morgan State University, Baltimore.

Technical Assistance Program, Fisk University, Nashville, Tennessee.

Center for Economic and Social Research, Prairie View A&M University, in College Station, Texas.

Rural Development Center, University of Maryland, Eastern Shore, in Princess Anne.

Public Administration Department, North Carolina Central University, Durham.

Technical Assistance Programs at University of Arkansas at Pine Bluff, Virginia State University in Petersburg, and Xavier University of Louisiana, in New Orleans.

are the internship and outreach activities at Morgan State University, in Baltimore, and an exhibit at New Mexico's Santa Fe Indian School, which was the result of the graduate planning students' community involvement.

In the May 1989 *Planning,* Jennifer Stern focused on an "academic program" that advocates community empowerment in her article "Pratt to the Rescue." The Pratt Institute Center for Community and Environmental Development in New York has been the catalyst for many community development projects.

The Community Information Exchange (CIE), in Washington, D.C., 202-628-2981 offers a comprehensive computerized source of information regarding community economic development and housing. As of June 1994, CIE lists 36 university-based programs in its technical assistance database. Twelve of the schools in the database are highlighted below. This list shows that universities across the country play a wide variety of roles in community development.

The Center for Organizational and Community Development (COCD), University of Massachusetts, Amherst. The COCD provides information, research, and referral for individual citizens, community organizations, university personnel, and elected officials.

The Center for Neighborhood Development, College of Urban Affairs, Cleveland State University, Cleveland, Ohio. The center was founded to provide training to assist neighborhood organizations in developing housing, business, and commercial revitalization projects.

The Kansas Cooperative Extension Services, Community Development Unit, Kansas State University, Manhattan. The unit provides training, information research, and referral for local community leaders in the areas of economic development, organization and leadership development, and local government.

The Community Development Group, School of Design, North Carolina State University, Raleigh. The group provides off-site technical assistance, such as architectural design and planning assistance to community organizations and nonprofit organizations in North Carolina. The group also operates as the field placement program for the graduate architecture program, at North Carolina State University.

The Center for Health Services, Vanderbilt University, Nashville, Tennessee. The center provides information, research, and referral regarding toxic waste, maternal/infant health, and community health. The center is recognized for its "action research." Students at Vanderbilt are given the opportunity to work with local agencies and organizations on a variety of environmental and health care issues.

The Center for Urban and Regional Affairs (CURA), University of Minnesota, Minneapolis. CURA supports University of Minnesota faculty and students to undertake research projects relating to community issues—housing, employment, environment and energy, human services, land use, minorities, planning and public affairs.

The Center for Community Development, University of Delaware, Wilmington. The center specializes in packaging housing rehabilitation projects, maintaining and developing small businesses, analyzing the availability of neighborhood goods and services, and promoting community development corporations and cooperatives.

The Center for Economic Development, University of New Orleans, Louisiana. The services included in the center include research, planning, business consulting and management training in market demand analysis and loan packaging. The center focuses on training for individuals, businesses, community agencies, and economic development organizations to generate and maintain employment opportunities in southern Louisiana.

North Dakota State University Extension Service, North Dakota State University, Fargo. This extension program provides community development assistance to rural areas. The university primarily offers information, research, referral, training, and on-site technical assistance through local county agents.

City College Architectural Center, New York, N.Y. The center provides preliminary architectural and planning assistance, generally to low-income, community-based organizations and individuals.

The Colorado Center for Community Development, University of Colorado at Denver. Using its own resources, the university provides education and technical assistance to rural small towns, low-income minority communities, and community-based organizations.

The Partnership for Rural Improvement, Washington State University, Pullman. The partnership, made up of educational institutions, public agencies, and community activists, collaborates to stimulate community development in the State of Washington.

HELP FROM HUD

HUD has a regular technical assistance program that receives competitive applications from technical assistance providers throughout the country. All universities are encouraged to participate.

In 1991 and 1992, HUD provided another program—the Historically Black Colleges and Universities Cooperative Agreement Application Program. During the 1993 round of HUD competitions, the following universities were funded for physical development projects:

- **Jackson State University, Jackson Mississippi**. The University will acquire and rehabilitate 40 vacant homes. The project will provide low- to moderate-income individuals the opportunity to own their own homes.

- **Lincoln State University, Chester County, Pennsylvania.** Funding from HUD will be used to construct a Community Learning Center to conduct various programs for neighborhood residents. University faculty and students will participate in the programs offered through the center. Programs will include courses in entrepreneurial training, job skills training, leadership training and family literacy training.

- **University of Arkansas at Pine Bluff.** UAPB will enter into a joint venture with Pine Bluff's municipal government to assist in the implementation of community reinvestment activities.

- **Coppin State College, Baltimore.** Coppin State has formed a partnership with the Neighborhood Housing Services, Inc. (i.e., a nonprofit organization) and the City of Baltimore, to enhance its adjacent community, Coppin Heights.

- **Bennett College, Greensboro, North Carolina.** The college community development corporation (CDC) has developed a relationship with the City of Greensboro to stimulate economic development in the adjacent community. The CDC will increase

homeownership by subsidizing the development of eight houses
and renovation of an existing building as an entrepreneurial
training center.

- **Norfolk State University, Norfolk, Virginia.** Norfolk State is
  acting as a catalyst for community development and neighborhood revitalization in the adjacent Brambleton Community.
  Activities include the renovation of eight houses to provide
  homeownership for low-income residents, the provision of
  research and training related to new technologies in the construction of affordable housing, and the development of a partnership with the Plumb Line Ministries, a community development corporation.

- **Southern University and A&M College, Baton Rouge, Louisiana.** The Southern University Community Development Partnership will conduct four major activities: the provision of assistance to first-time home buyers; the acquisition and rehabilitation of substandard residential properties in Baton Rouge; and
  the development of a community development housing organization.

- **Central State University, Wilberforce, Ohio.** The university will
  use HUD funds as seed money to initiate a two-year program to
  stimulate economic development through neighborhood revitalization, affordable and fair housing initiatives in Greene County,
  Ohio.

- **LeMoyne Owen College, Memphis, Tennessee.** The university
  will promote economic development through the development
  of a business incubator. Businesses will receive assistance in the
  development of business plans, a variety of shared services and
  a revolving loan fund.

OTHER SOURCES OF FUNDS

The Structured Employment/Economic Development Corporation,
commonly known as SEEDCO, is working with several historically
black colleges and universities. In 1990, SEEDCO, which is located in
New York (212-473-0255), received funds from the Ford Foundation and
the Charles Stewart Mott Foundation to assist in the initiation of a

program to help historically black colleges and universities in the Southeast form partnerships with adjacent communities through the creation of nonprofit community development corporations (CDCs). During the first program year, SEEDCO assisted in the development of four partnerships: Clark Atlanta University, in Atlanta; Johnson C. Smith University, in Charlotte, North Carolina; Jackson State University, in Jackson, Mississippi; and Xavier University of Louisiana, in New Orleans. Winston-Salem State University in North Carolina and Hampton University in Virginia have become SEEDCO partners, and R.J. Reynolds Tobacco Company supports these newer partnerships.

HUD also has a community development work study program, which has produced a cadre of well-prepared professionals over the past 20 years. HUD solicits grant applications from institutions of higher education, or through areawide planning organizations or states. The program purpose is:

> . . . providing assistance to economically disadvantaged and minority students who participate in community development work study programs and are enrolled in full-time graduate or undergraduate programs in community and economic development, community planning or community management, or other related fields of study. Related fields include public administration, urban management, urban planning and exclude social and humanistic fields such as law, economics, psychology, education and history.

Students enrolling in this program gain a master's degree and two years of progressive professional experience. The student is also exposed to resources and a network of professionals who should prove invaluable for future professional growth and development. Schools in the following HUD regions received awards for the 1992-94 program:

REGION I
New Hampshire College

REGION III
Carnegie Mellon University
University of Baltimore
Morgan State University

REGION IV
Eastern Kentucky University
Clemson University
Triangle COG (Durham, North Carolina)
      University of North Carolina
      North Carolina Central University
Alabama A&M University

REGION V
University of Wisconsin
University of Illinois
Mankato State University

REGION VI
North Central Texas COG
      University of North Texas
      University of Texas at Arlington
Iowa State University

REGION X
Eastern Washington University

THE ROLE OF APA

The American Planning Association has traditionally convened panels at its annual conference to highlight the efforts of academic institutions. In 1992, in Washington, D.C., the HUD Deputy Undersecretary for Intergovernmental Relations moderated a panel providing clear evidence of university involvement in community development. The panel, "Helping Minority Communities Plan," demonstrated how academic institutions could provide technical assistance, from both faculty and students, to help minority communities plan their futures and develop economically.

At the 1993 APA conference in Chicago, a panel entitled "Achieving Social and Economic Equity in Community Planning—The University's Role," discussed how universities assist in achieving social and economic equity in community planning in large cities, metropolitan areas, small towns, and rural communities.

The common theme that runs through the three university-based programs discussed by the panel is that the research priorities are community driven. While they are funded through a variety of sources—federal grant programs, university/institutional support, and private foundations—each program looks to the adjacent community for the determination of how it can best serve that community.

The University of Illinois at Chicago's Center for Urban Economic Development (CUED) was founded in 1978. The annual report characterizes CUED as "a multifaceted policy research and technical assistance organization with a diversified base of support." Through the provision of technical assistance to community based organizations, CUED has assisted in making economic development a central policy issue in Chicago. The CUED philosophy is reflected in its director's belief that "decisions about neighborhoods should be made with grass-roots organizations."

It is interesting to note the "sister" campus of the University of Illinois, at Urbana-Champaign, is also undertaking a grass-roots initiative, through its Department of Urban and Regional Planning. The planning department's East St. Louis Action Research project combines applied research, teaching, and public service.

In 1989, the Department of Community Planning and Urban Studies at Alabama A&M University used its extensive community development experience to organize the Community Development Technical Assistance Program. CDTAP received requests to undertake neighborhood organization and project development in Huntsville and Athens, Alabama. Through on-site peer-to-peer assistance, informational and organizational sessions with target neighborhood residents, community newsletters/bulletins, and leadership and management training workshops/seminars, CDTAP was successful in developing two viable neighborhood corporations over a three-year period.

Using its effective community outreach program and popular community development work-study internship program, the Institute for Urban Research at Morgan State University developed the Community Development Resource Center (CDRC) in 1991. The center was specially developed to provide technical assistance to community-based organizations in the Baltimore metropolitan area, the city, and the five surrounding counties. CDRC provides this assistance through three programs that are directly responsive to requests from the metropolitan community.

The American Planning Association continues to promote university outreach efforts through its publications and conference/workshop forums. In the May 1994 issue of *Planning*, Lawrence Muhammad's article, "Applied Academics," profiled Louisville professor John Gilderbloom and focused on the University of Louisville's program, Housing and Neighborhood Development Strategies (HANDS). The HANDS project has targeted Louisville, Kentucky's Russell neighborhood to provide job training, and social and housing assistance. In the article, Gilderbloom summarized what university collaborators with community development partners might expect. HANDS, said Professor Gilderbloom, took him "from confrontational politics to partnerships; you push for things where everyone wins."

SUMMARY

During this decade of transition into the 21st century, universities and community development partners (community-based organizations, religious institutions, financial institutions, public agencies, private entrepreneurs, nonprofits) are confronted with major issues, including limited resources, technological advances, a need to provide more responsive education/training, and the demand for applied research.

Resources are limited. This seems to be universally accepted. Thus, the reality of the limits on monetary, human, and other resources should stimulate community development partners to be creative/innovative— develop partnerships and alternative ways to collaborate to resolve community development issues and grapple with limited resources by maximizing existing resources and leveraging financial and in-kind contributions from other community development partners. The university can take a leadership role in fostering this kind of collaboration between and among community development partners.

Technological advances are prayed for and hoped for, but often feared. As technology advances dramatically, the costs of such advances and limited availability impact access for the "person on the street." Universities which have traditionally been on the cutting edge of technological advances can provide training and access to community development partners, easing the transition into the use of technology.

More responsive education/training is required. Community development partners have neither the time nor the funds to take three or four years to pursue college degrees. Universities are finding ways to make education and training available through continuing education, weekend programs, and evening programs, as well as short-term institutes, seminars, and workshops.

The demand for applied research negates the ivy tower "research for the sake of research." Universities can no longer afford to ponder the issues of the day for years and years. Community-based organizations are "tied" of being studied to death. The demand for information and research that will move the community along and allow community development partners to pursue practical agendas must be given serious consideration. Applied research efforts are proliferating at universities across the country.

In the development of a collaborative effort toward community development, universities should keep in mind a portion of Charles Abrams's comprehensive definition of community:

> . . . Community, finally, is that mythical state of social wholeness in which each member has his place and in which life is regulated by cooperation rather than by competition and conflict. It has had brief and intermittent flowerings through history but always seems to be in decline at any given historical present. Thus community is that which each generation feels it must rediscover and re-create. (*The Language of Cities: A Glossary of Terms*, 1971.)

Elva E. Tillman is the project director for the Community Development Resource Center in the Institute for Urban Research, at Morgan State University, in Baltimore. She received her Master of Urban and Regional Planning from Virginia Polytechnic Institute and State University, and a Juris Doctorate from the University of Maryland. She has served as the chief of the Capital Improvement Programming Section of the Baltimore City Department of Planning; administrator of the Housing and Community Development Office in Howard County, Maryland; project director for the Development Training Institute; associate at Piper/Marbury Law Firm; special assistant city solicitor for the Baltimore City Department of Law; and coordinator of the City and Regional Planning Program at Morgan State University.

Rural Diversity:
Challenge for a Century

By Nancy Benzinger Brown, AICP,

Mark Lapping, AICP, and Edward J. Blakely[1]

Crises provoke responses. While crises provide opportunities for change, immediate problems are often so overwhelming that broader issues and longer-term solutions fall by the wayside. In planning, too, long-term solutions are often sacrificed for short-term "fixes." A recent example is southern Florida where Hurricane Andrew left a virtually blank canvas for planners. Some plans were launched, but it was clear that the greatest concern after the hurricane was housing those without shelter. Rebuilding rather than replanning resulted. As the Dade County planning director told *Planning* magazine, "If you don't have a roof over your head, you don't care what the 10-year or 20-year plan is."

Nevertheless, as planners we have a responsibility to go beyond today's problems, no matter how pressing they may be, to focus on the long-term. Only in this way will structural problems be addressed in a coherent manner.

APA's Agenda for America's Communities resulted from a crisis—the riots in Los Angeles. It began as an "urban agenda," and there are many that would argue that the plight of the inner city is the single most critical issue facing planning today. Yet, here is what Norman Krumholz said in that same January 1993 issue of *Planning*:

What happens in one jurisdiction affects its neighbors' air, water, health—and wallets—now more than ever before. . . . We can no longer look the other way and pretend that what happens next door is not our business.

Krumholz's remarks appear to emphasize the need for social equity planning in all communities, not just urban areas.

Rural areas are a part of the mix of America, and they are changing. They are affected by and affect suburban and urban areas. Rural areas must be considered in any discussion of a planning agenda for America that focuses on the importance of social equity and diversity and asks how planners may foster diversity. This paper presents a rationale for a rural agenda, examines the face of rural America, summarizes the planning issues that face rural America, and suggests specific actions that may be taken by the American Planning Association and individual planners to promote rural diversity.

RATIONALE FOR A RURAL AGENDA

Rural and urban areas not only have an impact on each other, but are both adversely impacted by the ever-growing centrifugal force exerted by suburban areas. The suburbs are the growth nodes that are drawing jobs, residences, stores, plants, and offices away from both urban and rural areas. They are becoming the consumers of the best and leaving urban and rural areas to cope with the poor, the less well-educated, and the underemployed and unemployed. Social equity in America can never be achieved by allowing the reverse ghettoization of cities and rural areas.

In rural areas there is some hope, primarily because the scale of rural America is so much more socioeconomically manageable. Problems, while challenging, can often be addressed if the community is willing to engage them.

Perhaps ironically, another rural advantage is lack of choice. People are forced to interact—to shop at the only grocery store, patronize the only movie theater. Instead of a variety of schools, rural parents and children have limited options. No matter where they live, all students go to the one high school in the county.

Dimensions of Rural Diversity

What are the problems of diversity that planners need to address in rural areas? Are there a greater proportion of minorities, poor, female heads of households, and elderly in the rural areas? What is the makeup of minorities in the United States? Where are Native Americans? The full report of the 1990 Census will eventually provide the best answers to these questions, but there are data available that point to some answers.

According to the Census Bureau's *Poverty in the United States: 1991*

> As has historically been the case, the nonmetropolitan poverty rate in 1991 (16.1 percent) was higher than that for metropolitan areas (13.7 percent) . . . a larger proportion of poor Blacks lived in nonmetropolitan areas (18.2 percent) than nonpoor Blacks (13.9 percent). [pp. xii-xiii]

It appears that, while more of those classified as black live in the central cities, those in the nonmetropolitan (rural) areas are worse off economically. Poverty areas, those minor civil divisions in rural areas, have a poverty rate of 20 percent or greater. While 60 percent of the poor live in central cities, 26 percent live in rural areas with far fewer resources and services. [p. xiii]

In the Northeast and Midwest, nonmetropolitan poor are mostly white. In the South—where 19.8 percent are below poverty—39.9 percent of blacks, 35.9 percent of Hispanics, and 15.2 percent of whites outside metropolitan areas are below poverty.

Blacks (25.5 percent) and Hispanics (29.7 percent) have much higher poverty levels than whites (14.4 percent) in the West.

However, scale is also the enemy. The population of rural areas is seldom large or diverse enough to support a variety of services, many of which would promote social equity. An African-American cultural center, for example, is much more likely to exist in an urban area. Rural communities are often hard pressed to support even the necessary infrastructure to provide minimum living standards—clean water, decent housing, adequate medical care, respectable schools.

Rural communities have a very narrow leadership base, often inherited or merited by community position, such as the small town banker or hardware store owner. When people are too poor or too poorly educated to have concerns beyond survival, it is critical for those in a position to make decisions—like planners—to find ways to bring all parts of the community into the process and to broaden and democratize the leadership base.

Some rural communities are beginning to realize that they cannot be successful without bringing the bottom up. An Agenda for America's Communities can never be successful until it has impacted the vast rural plains of the Midwest and the mountains of West Virginia, the mesas of the southwest and the Mississippi Delta region, as well as urban Los Angeles or Boston or Chicago.

Race and ethnicity play a role in shaping the lives of small town citizens. From primarily black communities in the Mississippi Delta, to Mexican-American communities along the border, to golden age Florida, to Rhode Island Portuguese-speaking communities, to Native American areas in the Southwest, small towns present an amazing variety. Any policy that encourages social equity in rural America should not result in the loss of racial or cultural variety, but rather should encourage it in a cooperative society.

To achieve a climate where laws and processes and social interaction support equality, small towns must pursue an agenda that promotes interaction and education of the public. Knowledge eases fears. While over the years many large cities have erupted into violence, in part because of feelings of rootlessness and isolation, small towns force personal interaction between ages, races, and ethnic groups. But control and fear in small towns can still wreak havoc. A lack of options in education and work, lack of mobility, and lack of income perpetrates vicious cycles of poverty, poor health, and low educational attainment that can persist for generations.

Before considering the key points in constructing an agenda that includes rural America, it is important to understand the true face of rural America.

REAL RURAL AMERICA

In some ways, rural America is still shrouded in myth. Many urbanites and suburbanites still see rural Americans as neo-Jeffersonian, rugged individualists who live largely safe and trouble-free lives amid the natural beauty of the hinterlands. Nothing could be further from the truth. Rural Americans, compared with those who live in urban areas, are more likely to be poor, less well-served by medical and other health services, less educated, more isolated from economic and social opportunities, and persistently at a disadvantage in accessing governmental, educational, and technological expertise.

Behind the facade of rural stability and tranquility are families and communities occupying some of the worst housing in the nation, heavily dependent upon transfer payments, living with outdated or even nonexistent infrastructure, such as water and sewage systems, and with fewer and fewer choices in terms of transportation and social service provision.

While this was not always the case, it is certainly true today that rural people have gone, to paraphrase historian John Shover, from being the first majority to becoming "the last minority." The end of federal revenue sharing and the recent round of deregulation have reduced further the range and scope of services for rural people as well as the capacity of many local governments to address important problems.

A second myth is the belief that the majority of small town and rural Americans are farmers. Indeed, less than one-tenth of all of those employed in such areas work in agriculture. Manufacturing, trade and sales, and services are far larger components of the rural economy than is farming. Closely related to this myth is the belief that the U.S. Department of Agriculture (USDA) is the federal rural agency in the same way that Housing and Urban Development (HUD) looks after the interests of the cities. The importance of USDA to rural areas is, like farming in general, in decline. Other federal bureaucracies, like Health and Human Services or Commerce, are growing in their influence in terms of policies and programs that affect rural places.

A third myth is the purported moral superiority of rural Americans. From the time of Jefferson to today, we have tended to view rural people as simple, honest, trustworthy, democratic, and fair-minded. In short, "country people" embody the very best of American values.

This sentiment has worked its way into the popular culture of the nation. John-Boy Walton, *Mayberry R.F.D.*, and *Green Acres* are the controlling images we have of rural people, and that—too often—rural people have of themselves. The power and pervasiveness of the moral superiority myth often prevents us from seeing rural people as real, and rural areas and small towns the way they often are. It masks the conflict, struggles, and divisions exacerbated by decades of neglect.

As with the rest of the nation, rural America is divided along gender, racial, ethnic, and age cleavages. Achieving equity in such areas is notably difficult. There is a narrow base of opportunity and a tradition-al unwillingness to deal with conflict and division because human relations are more personal and contact tends to be characterized by face-to-face interactions. There is increasing impoverishment (especially among women who are sole heads of households), aging, and polariza-tion of economic growth in many such regions.

With these facts in mind, an agenda for America that includes consider-ation of rural communities must incorporate certain principles and deal with specific issues. APA must:

- Recognize the interdependence of urban and rural areas. The problems of one cannot be adequately addressed without con-sideration of the other.

- Recognize that rural problems have a way of becoming urban issues, and that urban problems expand into the countryside too often.

- Encourage development of leaders from all races, ages, ethnic groups, and both genders.

- Explore the opportunities technology provides to educate and train, as well as to provide employment for rural areas.

- Reward communities that achieve high standards of diversity, whether urban, suburban, or rural.

- Recognize that the thin balance between an ecologically sound and environmentally balanced America rests on the intersection between urban and rural areas. If America is to be environmen-tally sustainable, rural areas must be.

- Understand the critical link between food production, resource development, and rural community survival.

- Recognize that the desired quality of small town life is a metaphor for the best of American values—honesty, frugality, human scale, and entrepreneurship.

RURAL ISSUES

With these principles in mind, what are the barriers to rural diversity? What rural issues must be addressed? For rural America, the issues range from a lack of financial resources and infrastructure to a lack of tools that fit rural areas. Planners need to be taught how to deal with the challenges of rural areas. These include: rural funding, skills for planners, regional perspectives, existing planning and zoning systems, rural areas as America's dump, and economic development. These principles can lead to an action agenda for APA.

Funding

The question of funding is significant. Social equity is difficult to achieve without economic equity. Jobs are less available and less well-paid in rural areas. Often new business and industry are reluctant to locate in rural areas which lack an adequate infrastructure. Will the information highway ever reach rural America? Only if funding is fairly disbursed.

Rural areas are usually at the mercy of state and federal funding agencies for any significant improvements in local infrastructure. Through improved infrastructure comes better jobs, and then better education from a higher tax base. Should APA advocate funding formulas that equalize the opportunities, as far as possible, of urban, rural, and suburban areas?

Schools are one example. Should infrastructure funds be focused on large urban areas where projects serve a larger client base, or should they be focused on areas that are the neediest, often rural areas? Should infrastructure investments be targeted only to those areas that choose growth—and have the ability to accommodate it? Perhaps we need a separate rural funding bank or agency composed of elements of HUD, USDA, Commerce, and Rural Development Association (RDA)—another Economic Development Administration (EDA) with a rural focus.

Planning Skills

Very little attention is given to rural or regional planning in current planning curricula. Few regional planners even exist anymore. Yet many planners end up serving as the "only lonely" in rural areas and small towns. Many planning commissioners in rural areas serve without any staff at all.

These planners and planning commissioners are the least likely to be able to take advantage of continuing education opportunities such as conferences and workshops. They find it very difficult to be absent from their communities, even if they could find the funding to travel and pay conference fees. APA needs to be able to provide these planners with tools and skills that they can use to promote social equity, and to work with the Association of Collegiate Schools of Planning to encourage planning academics to consider rural community needs as important.

Regional Perspectives

At one time, regional planning tried to come to grips with some very significant rural questions. Currently planners, and even elected officials, are beginning to realize that many planning problems must be addressed at the regional level. Waste disposal is but one example. A regional approach may be able to address equity issues that cannot easily be resolved at the local level.

A classic example of regional planning is the Appalachian Regional Commission (ARC). Rightly or wrongly, ARC decided that the most significant need of the region was for roads, and so they built roads for residents and for industries and businesses. The Lower Mississippi River Delta Commission, chaired by then-Gov. Bill Clinton, examined and attempted to address the shocking conditions of the region. The Tennessee Valley Authority (TVA), established as a regional agency, has neglected regional planning. But recently there has been a revival of interest in planning for the region, and TVA is completing a regional economic development strategy for the Tennessee River, considered to be TVA's first regional plan since 1937.

Development districts and councils of government are types of subregional planning agencies that often include rural areas. These agencies may provide opportunities for expanded consideration of regional issues. In many states, volatile issues such as waste are being dealt with at a regional scale. These issues require special use regional plans but there may be no requirement for overall regional plans.

It may be time to consider the development of regional human and natural resource agencies across the nation for rural America. Such agencies could be sources of technical support and funding for rural areas to deal with a wide variety of regional issues.

Zoning in Rural Areas

Zoning may be well suited to achieving suburban goals, such as maintaining high property values by separating uses economically as well as functionally. Zoning inhibits rather than promotes social interaction of various economic groups. It is an urban tool and not very useful for future rural development. But rural communities and rural planners have adopted criteria designed for urban and suburban areas—large lots, strict delineation of uses in zones, distance requirements for undesirable land uses. We need to fashion new criteria and land-use approaches, such as performance zoning criteria, tailored specifically to preserve, enhance, and develop rural places.

In many rural areas, there is much wider tolerance of a variety of land uses. This is but a modern variant of the much honored land-use integration of the classic American village. In the new town of Thomas Village, Virginia, higher cost residences share a subdivision with subsidized housing, a small business strip, and an access road to an industrial park. There is no perceived conflict of uses. The new modular or mobile home that would be considered repugnant to suburbanites may be welcomed in a rural area. Often there are no other options.

Small lots, shared housing, mobile home subdivisions, and a number of other alternatives can be encouraged by performance zoning for their cost advantages and for their ability to allow more rural residents to achieve decent, safe, and sanitary housing.

Rural Areas as America's Dump

Rural areas are most often the location of regional waste facilities, nuclear plants, toxic dumps, and most other facilities with major negative impacts. Poor rural communities, often those with large minority populations, are disproportionately the sites of such facilities.

In some situations, such as prison location, communities will volunteer for and even compete for such facilities. This is often a clear sign of economic desperation. In most cases, particularly where health and property values are concerned, such facilities are violently rejected by the general public.

However, America cannot exist without prisons, landfills, power generating plants and all the other NIMBYs. It is critical to develop a planning process that ensures rural areas are not required to take more than their fair share of such facilities. Any plan for locating NIMBYs should also include techniques for lowering the impact, both short-term and long-term, of the facility.

Economic Diversification

Economic development is a real concern in rural communities. There are no longer enough "cut and sew" factories or smokestacks to go around in rural America. They have moved to Mexico, Asia, and the Caribbean. Few new high-wage factories are looking for sites, and those high-wage industries that do locate in rural areas are unlikely to use much local labor. On the average, each community can attract a new industrial plant every 500 years. Of course, some communities are more successful than others, and many have no success at all.

As jolting as the loss of a major industry may be in a rural area, it may force economic diversification. Social equity can be more easily achieved in a stronger economy. Planners should encourage local economic diversification. Rural communities must diversify to the greatest extent possible. Some will develop as successful tourism or shopping destinations; others must determine another role within their region. Rural areas require technology infrastructure, such as telecommunications, air service, advanced warehousing and distribution facilities, as well as new investment in natural resource production and harvesting, to compete globally. Some rural areas may continue to serve their traditional, if changing, role in supplying natural resources for the region, nation, and world.

ACTION AGENDA FOR APA AND THE PROFESSION

Finally, there are specific actions that APA as an organization, and planners as professionals, can take to promote social equity in rural America as a part of APA's Agenda for America's Communities:

- Promote regional planning for urban, suburban, and rural areas. Rural planning can encourage the "fair share" allocation of problems, such as NIMBYs, and of opportunities, such as new businesses and industries. It can help avoid wasteful competition between areas in the region. For example, each community does not need its own industrial recruiter.
  Example: New Jersey State Plan

- Support equivalent funding to develop and redevelop urban and rural infrastructure—such as school systems, advanced telecommunication technology, abandoned military bases—which provides rural communities with a base for development.
  Examples: National telecommunication initiative
  Kentucky school funding

- Develop an integrated plan for a tiered system of medical care facilities from the rural clinic to the urban research hospital to enable each American to access the highest possible level of care.
  Example: A national, truly universal health care plan

- Support broad-based leadership training for quality rural communities and local capacity building through a specialized federal agency that can coordinate federal funding for rural areas.
  Examples: Iowa's Tomorrow's Leaders Today, Iowa State University
  TVA/National Rural Electric Cooperative Association's
  Southlink Program

- Promote the establishment of regional resource agencies with a focus on economic, human, and natural resource development. These 30 to 40 agencies would allocate rural funding.
  Examples: Appalachian Regional Commission
  Mississippi Delta Commission
  New England Regional Commission
  Tennessee Valley Authority

- Identify and develop ethnically and culturally diverse rural sites for recreation and tourism.
  Example: Wounded Knee, South Dakota

- Draft model national legislation for regional fair share of NIMBYs.
  Example: New York's Fair Share laws

- Foster state and national support (federal dollars) for improved education, health care, and jobs in the poorest 10 percent of counties across the nation.
  Example: Tennessee Valley Authority's Special Opportunity Counties

- Incorporate courses on small town, rural, and regional planning in university planning curriculum. Encourage study of rural planning issues by establishing a HUD Rural Studies Fellowship program similar to the HUD Urban Studies Fellowship program.
  Examples: Alabama A&M, California Polytechnic State University, Iowa State, Kansas State, University of California at Berkeley

- Develop training programs for planners that improve the citizen participation process by bringing planning to the people.
  Example: University of Wisconsin Cooperative Extension Program

- Advocate local land-use laws that allow better use of rural land resources for housing, employment, and economic development.
  Examples: Performance zoning, small lot subdivisions, shared housing zoning
  Vermont's Act 250 and 200

- Propose a national program of coordinated industrial development of rural areas by the states.
  Example: APA could adopt this as an initiative as a part of implementing the Agenda for America's Communities

- Encourage all states to adopt community achievement programs.
  Examples: California's Rural Renaissance
  Kansas's Pride Program

NOTES

1. The authors appreciate the assistance of John W. Keller, Planning Department, Kansas State University, and Douglas Hancock, School of Planning, College of Architecture & Planning, University of Tennessee, in preparing this paper.

SELECTED REFERENCES

Flora, Cornelia Butler, Jan L. Flora, Jacqueline D. Spears, Louis E. Swanson, with Mark B. Lapping and Mark L. Weinberg. 1992. *Rural Communities: Legacy & Change.* Colorado: Westview Press.

Lapping, Mark B., Thomas L. Daniels and John W. Keller. 1989. *Rural Planning & Development in the United States.* New York: Guilford Hall.

Nancy Benzinger Brown, AICP, has served as chair of APA's Small Town and Rural Planning Division and as president of the Tennessee Chapter of APA. During her 18 years with the Tennessee Valley Authority, she has provided technical assistance to a number of rural communities throughout TVA's seven-state region. Edward Blakely is currently dean of the Urban Studies School at the University of Southern California in Los Angeles. Formerly head of the planning program at the University of California at Berkeley, he has served as a member of the board of directors of the American Planning Association. Formerly founding dean of the Edward J. Bloustein School of Planning and Public Policy at Rutgers, Mark Lapping, AICP, is provost and vice-president for academic affairs and professor at the Muskie Institute of Public Affairs at the University of Southern Maine in Portland.

Index